A GALLERY
OF POISONE

GW00359718

Also by Adrian Vincent in Warner Books:

FATAL PASSIONS

A GALLERY OF POISONERS

Adrian Vincent

WARNER BOOKS

A *Warner* Book

First published in Great Britain in 1993
by Warner

A CIP catalogue record for this book is available
from the British Library.

ISBN 0 7515 0147 6

Typeset by Leaper & Gard Limited, Bristol
Printed in England by Clays Ltd, St Ives plc

Warner Books
A Division of
Little, Brown and Company (UK) Limited
165 Great Dover Street
London SE1 4YA

CONTENTS

THE MAN WHO HANGED HIMSELF

Frederick Seddon (1912)

On the surface, the Seddon ménage was one of those typical lower middle class households which were the backbone of Edwardian society. The paterfamilias, Frederick Henry Seddon was an insurance agent, the district superintendent for the Islington branch of the London and Manchester Industrial Company, and was a man who had about him an insufferable air of rectitude which he had no doubt acquired when he had been a chapel goer and teacher. His wife, Mary Ann, was a weak-willed woman who was completely subservient to her husband's tyrannical wishes – a not unusual situation in those days when the idea of women's rights was still being fiercely opposed by most men – including Frederick Seddon. The rest of the household consisted of Seddon's 73-year-old father and four children. There was also a servant named Mary Chater, a former mental nurse with a history of insanity in her family, who had the regrettable habit of throwing the crockery around whenever she had one of her 'turns'.

Apart from the somewhat hazardous business of going into the kitchen, when there was always the danger of being greeted by a piece of flying crockery, there would have been nothing particularly unusual about this household, had it not been for Frederick Seddon's character. A hard-working man, who seems to have served his company with extraordinary zeal, he had one major fault. He was mean to an almost insane degree.

His favourite occupation when at home was to count over his mounting store of gold coins, and to go over the accounts to see how much he could save on the housekeeping. It was this determination to save a few shillings where he could which was to lead him to the gallows, when he might possibly have saved himself by spending a little more on the coffin for the woman he had poisoned.

The story of Frederick Seddon's progress to the gallows begins when the family moved into 63 Tollington Park, London, N4, which Seddon had bought for £350, after having beaten the owner down on the price. It was by no means a gracious house, being one of those solidly built, early-Victorian houses that needed someone with a little taste and money to improve it. Needless to say, neither was forthcoming from Seddon, who was too busy totting up what the move had cost him to spend any money on the house. Being near to Holloway Prison, and in one of the more dreary streets in Finsbury Park, it was not exactly a coveted area in which to live. Whatever potentiality the house had inside was ruined by Seddon's parsimonious nature, with the result that the furniture he put in it had been bought on the cheap, making the house look worse than it actually was. It was in this house, less than a mile from Hilldrop Crescent, where Crippen had disposed of his wife less than three years earlier, that another murder was about to take place.

After turning one of the rooms into an office, for which he was given five shillings a week by his company, Seddon looked around for someone to take the unoccupied flat on the top floor. In the July of 1910, Miss Eliza Mary Barrow came to see the flat and agreed to take it. When she moved in she brought with her an engine driver named Robert Hook and his wife, who had both lodged with her at the previous address. The fourth member of the party was a six-year-old orphan boy named Ernie Grant, the nephew of Robert Hook, whose mother had been Miss Barrow's landlady until her death in 1908. The fact that Miss Barrow had more or less adopted Ernie was the one good thing that could be said for her. His sister, Hilda, went into an orphanage. By all accounts Miss Barrow was an unpleasant woman. She was forty-nine when she entered the Seddon household, when it soon became obvious to the Seddons that she was something of a drunken slut, whose favourite tipple was gin. She was a dirty and unkempt-looking woman, and was the very last person to have brought up the boy; why she bothered to try and do so remains something of a mystery. Like Seddon, she was also obsessed with money, hoarding her collection of gold coins in a cash box rather than putting it in the safe keeping of a bank.

The Hooks had hardly been in the house a week when Miss Barrow violently quarrelled with them and asked Seddon to order them to leave. Having already decided in that short space of time that Miss Barrow was a 'natural' victim to be milked of everything he could get his hands on, Seddon was only too happy to send the Hooks packing, leaving him free to fleece Miss Barrow without anyone asking him awkward questions.

Robert Hook must have suspected what was in his

mind, for his parting shot before they left was, 'I will defy you and a regiment like you to get her money in your hands.' He didn't know Seddon.

Seddon watched them go, trailing behind the small van that was carrying their modest belongings to their new home. Then he went back into the house to work out how he was going to part Miss Barrow from her money. As she was no simple-minded and trusting spinster, but a belligerent and suspicious woman who trusted no one, Seddon knew that he was faced with a formidable task.

It all proved much easier than Seddon had expected. Miss Barrow had a respect for her betters, and in many ways she saw Seddon as her social superior. He owned his own house, whereas Miss Barrow was only a tenant, and he had a well-paid job with a company he had worked for for more than twenty years. As befitting his position as a superintendent for his company, he was always well turned out, so that he gave Miss Barrow the impression that she was dealing with an important city gent, rather than what he actually was – a twopenny-halfpenny insurance agent. But what appealed to her most about him was that he never talked down to her, treating her as an equal who understood everything he was saying whenever he rattled off figures relating to percentages and dividends. Miss Barrow was just beginning to congratulate herself on being fortunate enough to be living at 63 Tollington Park, where so much sensible advice on her affairs was available, when Seddon struck with all the speed of a rattlesnake going in for the kill.

First there was the lease on the Buck's Head, a public

house that Miss Barrow owned in Camden, which he persuaded her to hand over to him for an annual income of fifty-two pounds. Then he persuaded her that it would be in her interests to let him have £1,600 in India stock in exchange for an annuity of £103. 4s. 5d. At the time, both parties expressed themselves well satisfied with the deal. Shortly after, Mrs Seddon gave birth to her fifth child, a baby girl she named Lily.

It was probably after these two deals that Seddon began to contemplate doing away with Miss Barrow, thereby saving him having to pay her more than £150 a year. What finally decided him was something that Miss Barrow let slip out during one of their conversations. According to her, she owned nearly £4,000 in gold sovereigns and paper money – most of it kept in the house.

Seddon's eyes watered with emotion as he thought of the money. 'That's a great deal of money to keep in the house, my dear,' he told Miss Barrow. 'I think perhaps you should hand it over to me for safe keeping.'

Miss Barrow wasn't *that* stupid, and for the time being the idea of getting his hands on the money had to remain only a tantalizing dream for Seddon. In the meantime he consoled himself with the £216 that Miss Barrow drew from the bank and presumably handed over to him for another of his annuities, as the money was never seen again.

Like so many Edwardian businessmen, Seddon was a great believer in the value of property, and it was at about this time he decided to get rid of his India stock. He received nearly £1,520, and with most of the proceeds of the sale he bought himself fourteen leasehold houses in

Coutts Road, Stepney. All of a sudden he was very much a man of property, a role he enjoyed, and to which he was to make particular reference at his trial.

From January 1911 until the August of that year, he refrained from killing Miss Barrow, for reasons which are not too difficult to establish. Ever since Miss Barrow had made it known to him that she had no wish to leave any money in her will to her relatives, Seddon had probably been angling for her to make a will in his favour, in exchange for a monthly payment until her death, which would then follow shortly afterwards. There was also the matter of the money Miss Barrow still had in the bank. When it became obvious that she had no intention of making out a will in his favour, there was still the possibility that she would make more withdrawals from the bank to add to the hoard she had in the house, which Seddon intended to steal the moment she was dead.

By the August it had become obvious that Miss Barrow was in no hurry to draw out any more money, and Seddon felt that he couldn't wait any longer. The time had now come for him to send her on her way.

On 5th August, he took the whole family and Miss Barrow away for a weekend in Southend. As this was very much out of character in a man who never took more than the one summer holiday a year, one can only assume that he wanted to get away for the weekend to concentrate his mind on the unpleasant task that lay ahead.

On their return home, Seddon sent his eldest daughter, Maggie, to the local chemist to buy some Mathers arsenical fly-papers. These were the same type that Mrs Maybrick was accused of using when she went on trial for the murder of her husband in 1889.

On the morning of Friday, 1st September, Miss Barrow was chatting with Mrs Seddon in the downstairs kitchen, when she suddenly complained that she was feeling unwell. Mrs Seddon helped her up to her bedroom, where she lay on the bed while Mrs Seddon made her a cup of tea, which Miss Barrow was unable to keep down. Mrs Seddon was not unduly alarmed, but as a precautionary measure, Dr Sworn, the family physician, was called in, and remained a regular visitor until her death on 13th September. With the laxity that seems to have been prevalent among general practitioners in those days, he did not bother to examine the body, having already diagnosed the cause of death as being from epidemic diarrhoea, though her symptoms could easily have been caused by arsenical poisoning.

In this writer's opinion, Miss Barrow's initial attack was not the result of being poisoned by Seddon, as many writers who have dealt with this case have assumed, but had been brought about by Miss Barrow's complete indifference to the most elementary rules of hygiene. It had been a sweltering hot August, which had lasted up until the September, and Miss Barrow's flat had been infested with flies which were forever settling on the food she had left out uncovered. To support this contention, Mrs Seddon was later to assert that Miss Barrow had had similar attacks of this nature before – long before Seddon had even considered poisoning Miss Barrow for her money.

What the first attack *did* do was to give Seddon the ideal opportunity to lace the liquid diet which Dr Sworn had advised; Valentine's meat juice, which he had prescribed, being particularly suitable for mixing with the arsenic that Seddon had extracted from the flypapers.

During the period that Miss Barrow was alive, Seddon had been careful to keep out of her way, except on the one occasion when he had gone up to see her, and found her more concerned with her financial affairs than with the state of her health. She did say, however, that she wanted to make sure that young Ernie and Hilda should get everything if anything happened to her.

'May I suggest you call in a solicitor,' Seddon had said.

Miss Barrow had agreed, and a will was duly drawn up, making Seddon her sole executor. His duties as such included holding on to Miss Barrow's personal possessions and the furniture until Ernie and Hilda were of age, when he was to sell everything and hand over the proceeds to the two children. This was an added bonus for Seddon, who could now go through her effects at leisure and help himself to what he wanted. As Miss Barrow had not itemized her personal belongings, Seddon intended eventually to take the lot.

After a woman had been in to lay out Miss Barrow, Seddon went along to see Mr Nodes, the undertaker, and told him that he had only £4.10s. to pay for the funeral.

'For that sum the deceased will have to be buried in a public grave,' the undertaker told him.

'Then there's the matter of my commission for

introducing the business,' Seddon had the audacity to say. 'Shall we say £3.17s. 6d. to include everything?'

Business was slack and Mr Nodes reluctantly shook hands on the deal. Understandably, as the late Miss Barrow's body was full of arsenic, Seddon was anxious to get her underground as soon as possible. 'I want the deceased to be buried tomorrow afternoon,' Seddon said. 'That means you'll have to remove the body this evening.'

Mr Nodes sighed. 'If you insist, Mr Seddon.'

Seddon had gone through Miss Barrow's effects in the morning, and had found two watches, a bracelet and some brooches. 'There's not much here,' Seddon told his wife and the charlady whom Seddon had insisted should be present. 'There will be very little for poor Ernie and Hilda.' It was surprising there was anything, as Seddon had already stolen the gold coins and whatever cash there had been.

Nearly three weeks after Miss Barrow had been buried, Seddon received a visit from Mr and Mrs Frank Vonderahe, Miss Barrow's nearest relatives. They were both in an angry mood, which was hardly surprising as Seddon had omitted to inform them of Miss Barrow's death, and, to make matters worse, Seddon was away on holiday when they had found out about her demise four days after the funeral, and then, having returned from holiday, kept putting them off until he had finally agreed to this meeting.

The interview was a stormy one, with Frank Vonderahe complaining bitterly that Miss Barrow had been buried in a public grave when he would gladly have paid the difference for a decent burial had he but been informed. Seddon coldly told them that he had written, and had, moreover, kept a copy of the letter, which he produced. Whether Seddon actually posted the original letter is highly debatable.

Seddon then began to discuss Miss Barrow's financial affairs. 'According to my reckoning, you owe me £1.1s. 10½d.,' Seddon said. 'She left exactly ten pounds in cash. From this I have deducted the expense of the funeral and Ernie's keep.' He produced a piece of paper from a drawer. 'You'll find it all itemized here.'

Frank Vonderahe angrily pushed the piece of paper aside. 'I know she kept a large amount of money in the house. What happened to it?'

'There was nothing,' Seddon said calmly. 'Only the ten pounds and her personal possessions which have been valued at sixteen pounds. Incidentally, I'm quite prepared to bring up Ernie.'

What prompted him to offer to look after Ernie? Was his cold heart moved at last by the plight of poor adenoidal Ernie, whom he had deprived of the one person willing to bring him up? Perhaps he saw the boy as a living example of his kindness and generosity to be pushed forward whenever someone accused him of being a skinflint. Or was it merely because the addition of one more to his family made very little difference to him in terms of hard cash, except for the cost of Ernie's clothing?

Frank then asked Seddon a number of probing questions which Seddon parried easily enough. 'Everything has been done in a perfectly legal manner,' he assured the Vonderahes. He then produced a copy of the will, which Frank scanned through.

'May we see the original of the will?' asked Frank.

'You may not,' Seddon retorted. 'The only person who has the right to do that is your brother, Percy, whom I believe disappeared some time ago.'

Why Seddon should have refused to show him the will is another puzzling factor in this case, especially as the copy had not been tampered with in any way. By refusing to show the will, which one could put down to Seddon being bloody-minded just for the sake of it, he merely increased the Vonderahes' growing suspicions, which they wasted no time in communicating to the police after they had left. On 15th November, an order was issued to exhume the body, and Dr Bernard Spilsbury, the pathologist, was called in to carry out the postmortem, together with Dr Willcock, the senior analyst to the Home Office.

Spilsbury had made his reputation with the case of Dr Crippen, in which his evidence had played a large part in putting the hangman's noose around Crippen's neck. The Seddon case was to take him one step further up the ladder of fame, his reputation unassailable until as late as 1932, when his evidence at the trial of Mrs Elvira Barney, accused of having shot her young lover, was torn to shreds by Sir Patrick Hastings.

In this case, however, he was able to prove beyond question that Miss Barrow's death had been caused by arsenical poisoning. A warrant was issued for the arrest of Seddon on 4th December, and he was taken into custody outside his own home that evening. His only

comments were, 'Absurd! What a terrible charge –
wilful murder! It is the first of our family that has ever
been charged with such a crime.'

On 15th January, Mrs Seddon was also arrested, merely
remarking, 'Very well', when the police came for her.

Why did the police arrest Mrs Seddon? And on what
evidence? There was none, beyond the fact that she had
happened to buy some fly papers, and that she had
cashed some cheques for Miss Barrow and had used a
false name when asked to sign for the money. However
faintly suspicious this might seem in the telling, it hardly
justified her being arrested – unless, of course, the police
assumed that as Seddon's wife, she had been privy to
everything that had gone on in the house.

The trial of Frederick Seddon and Mary Ann Seddon
began in the Old Bailey on the morning of 4th March
1912. All murder cases were highly dramatic affairs in
those days, with the prisoner's very life depending on
the outcome. This one, however, promised to be more
dramatic than most, with Marshall Hall appearing for
the defence, and the Attorney General, Sir Rufus Isaacs,
appearing for the Crown. Both men already had formidable reputations, especially Marshall Hall, who treated
the courtroom as a theatre in which he could display his
love for the legal pyrotechnics which were already
beginning to make him a household name. Sir Rufus
Isaacs, later to become Lord Reading, was a totally
different character. Cool and incisive in the courtroom,
his patrician features seldom showed anything like the
emotion of Marshall Hall when facing the jurors; he was
nevertheless a lethal prosecutor.

In the courtroom the spectators gazed at Seddon and wondered if he really was guilty as charged, as thousands of others had wondered in the past when they had gazed at the accused prisoner in the dock. The man they saw was bald-headed and sported a heavy moustache, and looked unassuming enough, as Dr Crippen had done in the dock. Unlike Crippen, though, Seddon's whole demeanour radiated an air of self-confidence and arrogance. It was this arrogance, coupled with his know-all attitude and his obvious contempt for everyone in the courtroom, which was to put the hangman's noose around his neck more surely than any of the actual evidence produced against him. As for Mrs Seddon, no one quite knew why she was standing in the dock, when it seemed obvious to everyone almost from the beginning of the trial that she was innocent.

The battle that was to follow between Marshall Hall and Sir Rufus Isaacs was held before Mr Justice Bucknill, whose uncontrollable tears before the court while delivering sentence on Frederick Seddon, were to provide one of the more famous courtroom stories involving a judge.

The fact that Miss Barrow died from arsenical poisoning was never in serious dispute. Once it had been established again for the benefit of the jurors, the question, as far as Marshall Hall was concerned, was not so much who administered the arsenic, but when it was taken and by what means. If he could establish that Miss Barrow had been ingesting the substance long before the Seddons were presumed to have poisoned her, there would be no case to answer, and the pair would be declared innocent.

Marshall Hall was not at his very best at this trial, perhaps because he knew that Seddon's manner and basic personality could all too easily sabotage any points he made in the prisoner's favour. Even so, there were moments when he must have caused the jurors to wonder if the Seddons were not innocent, after all.

From the beginning Marshall Hall tried to convince the jury that Miss Barrow was an arsenic eater, an addiction that was not uncommon in those days. To support this theory, he pointed out that a Royal Commission had already proven beyond doubt that arsenic was to be found in the roots of the hair of excessive beer drinkers. He was not suggesting that Miss Barrow was an excessive beer drinker, but that when arsenic was found in the roots of the hair, it was a clear indication that it had been in the body for a long time, as it took as much as twelve months to appear in the roots. Arsenic had been found in the roots of Miss Barrow's hair, thereby proving his point, he contended.

This was an ingenious theory and might have carried some weight with the jury, if Willcock, the analyst who had helped Bernard Spilsbury at the exhumation, had not come up with the answer. While in her coffin Miss Barrow's hair had become soaked with her own body fluids which contained arsenic. Marshall Hall had to begin again, this time quoting the case of the Styrian peasants from Hungary who were addicted to arsenic eating with no noticeable ill effects, though arsenic existed in the body for years. Was it not possible, Marshall Hall argued, that this is what had happened to Miss Barrow? Was it not possible that what she had really died of was epidemic diarrhoea, as had been stated on the death certificate?

The jury was obviously unconvinced.

Marshall Hall's strongest telling point came towards the end of the trial. 'Why,' he thundered, 'didn't Seddon, were he guilty of poisoning Miss Barrow, have the body cremated? He would have had no difficulty at all, especially as he had been given a certificate of death from natural causes.' A very good point, and one that Seddon must have wished he had thought of himself when making the funeral arrangements.

The case against Mrs Seddon was a weak one, as Mr Gervais Rentaul, her defence counsel, and even the judge himself, pointed out to the jury. It was based on two pieces of evidence that might or might not have proved that she was Seddon's willing accomplice. She was known to have cashed some of Miss Barrow's five pound notes for gold at various places, and signed for them with the false name and address of M. Scott of Evershott Road, and on one occasion she had bought some fly papers which she had put to soak in Miss Barrow's room, to keep away the flies.

When questioned about the false name and address she had given, Mrs Seddon said, 'Because the notes did not belong to me.'

'Then why did you not give Miss Barrow's name?' she was asked.

'Because I had no right to sign Miss Barrow's name.'

This rather baffling piece of confused morality was accepted merely as an example of Mrs Seddon's disarming frankness, and before she left the stand, it was obvious that she was going to be acquitted.

With Seddon it was a very different matter. There was no definite evidence against him to indicate that he had poisoned Miss Barrow, so the case against him was a purely circumstantial one. It was true that he was the only person to benefit from the death of Miss Barrow. But would a man in his position really murder for the amount of money involved? Seddon himself was to write after his trial:

> 'There was no motive for me to commit such a crime. I would have to be a greedy, inhuman monster, or to be suffering from a degenerate or deranged mind, as I was in good financial circumstances, 21 years in the same employ, a good position, a good home with every comfort, a wife, 5 children and an aged father (73) depending on me, my income just on £15 a week . . .'

The rest of the letter set out to prove that by murdering Miss Barrow he would have been gaining only twenty-six shillings a week.

The case for the Crown was based on the seemingly unlikely premise that Seddon had murdered for so little. Having established the motive and the opportunity to commit the murder, the Attorney General called no less than forty-five witnesses, who all spoke with horror and incredulity of Seddon's incredible greed for money. In all the examples of Seddon's greed and meanness that were made known to the court, none was more damning than the undertaker's account of how Seddon had haggled over the price of the burial and extracted a trifling commission from him, while arranging for Miss Barrow to be buried in a pauper's grave. From all their accounts of Seddon, the jurors were able to build up a picture of a ruthless and greedy man who was so pathologically obsessed with money that he was obviously capable of murder if it meant putting a few extra shillings in his pocket.

The jury was out for exactly an hour before they returned with their verdict. Mrs Seddon was found not guilty and acquitted, while Seddon was found guilty as charged. Seddon leaned over and kissed his wife when he heard that she had been declared innocent, and then turned to face the judge while she was led away in tears.

When asked if he had anything to say before sentence of death was passed on him, Seddon made a long speech in which he protested his innocence. He then gave the judge a Masonic sign, while saying, 'I declare before the Great Architect of the Universe, I am not guilty, my Lord . . .'

This appeal for clemency from one Freemason to another had a marked effect on the judge, who answered Seddon in a faltering voice that became charged with emotion when he made an indirect reference to Seddon's use of the Masonic sign. 'You and I know we belong to the same brotherhood. But our brotherhood does not encourage crime – on the contrary, it condemns it. I pray you make your peace with the Great Architect of the Universe . . .' He was in tears when he ordered Seddon to be taken to a place of execution and hanged by the neck until he was dead.

Seddon was hanged on 28th April 1912. Instead of sinking into obscurity as the shamed wife of the executed poisoner, Mrs Seddon bounced back into the headlines three times, the first time being when she remarried within weeks of her husband's execution. The next occasion was when she said in a 'confession' in the *Weekly Dispatch* that she had seen Seddon poison Miss Barrow, but had kept silent because he had threatened her with a revolver. The third occasion was when she admitted in an article in *John Bull* that her confession for the *Dispatch* was a farrago of nonsense which she had concocted purely because she had needed the money.

As for poor Ernie and Hilda, it is to be hoped that life was kinder to them in the future than it had been in the past.

But perhaps the last words in this case belong to Seddon who remained true to his nature to the very last. Just before his death, he was informed that his house had just been sold for less than its market value. 'That's finished it!' he groaned.

He must be the only murderer in history who went to the gallows more concerned with the poor price his property had fetched than with his impending doom.

A VERY FINE COOK

Tillie Gburek (USA 1921)

Like all large cities, Chicago had its ethnic communities, who lived, worked and died in one of the run-down areas of the city. Life was not easy in these ghettos which had sprung up after America had first opened her doors around 1848 to receive the great flood of refugees from Europe. They had come with high hopes of finding a rewarding new life in the States, merely to find themselves only marginally better off than they had been in the Old Country. The quarter known in Chicago as Little Poland was no better or worse than any other of the sections of the city where the refugees had made their homes, except that most of the small businesses in Little Poland were given over to the rag trade, an industry in those days where women slaved from dawn to dusk, producing garments for the lower end of the market.

For most of the women who worked in these factories, the only way of escape was to get married through one of the marriage brokers operating in the area. Generally, if they were young and attractive, the marriage broker was able to find them a husband, whereupon the bride exchanged the serfdom of the sewing machine for that of the kitchen.

Tillie Gburek was young, but not by any stretch of the imagination could she be called pretty. In fact, it would not be unfair to say she looked more like a stevedore in drag than a woman in the full bloom of youth. In all other respects, Tillie was a normal, full-blooded woman, and it was therefore only natural that she should think of finding herself a husband. As was the custom in Little

Poland, she went to see one of the marriage brokers in the neighbourhood.

'So you want to find yourself a husband, my dear,' the broker said. She looked at Tillie as she sat there, in her shapeless sweater, with muscular arms akimbo, her peasant-like face flushed with expectation. Being a woman who disliked turning away business, she nailed an encouraging smile on her lips. 'I'm sure I can do something for you. That'll be $50, please.'

The prospective husband the broker came up with was John Mitkiewitz, a man who was far more interested in finding himself a good cook, rather than some flighty and unreliable sexy-looking girl who was liable to stray. As it happened, Tillie Gburek was the ideal partner, for if there was one thing she could do well, it was to cook a good meal. The happy couple were united in 1886, and though it could hardly be called the marriage of the year in Little Poland, it seemed a sensible marriage to those who knew Tillie and John.

Tillie was twenty-one when she married, and despite the odds being against her, with so many attractive girls around in the neighbourhood, she managed to hold on to her husband for the next twenty years, mainly because John Mitkiewitz needed Tillie to support him, being a feckless drunk, with a marked disinclination to work. Faced with the necessity of being the breadwinner for most of the time, Tillie had continued to work at the sweat shop for many years, with little or no support from her husband.

In 1911 something happened which was to change Tillie's whole life. Her boss, being a man who liked to see his staff working themselves to death, had occasion one day to start shouting at her for not working fast enough. Instead of bowing her head meekly while her boss ranted at her, Tillie rose from her machine and planted a hamlike fist in his face. It did not matter at first that Tillie was out of work as soon as her boss had recovered consciousness. Overnight she had become the heroine of the neighbourhood – that is with the exception of her husband, who merely scolded her for losing her job. Tillie's answer was to floor him with a single blow.

'Go out and get yourself a job for a change,' she shouted at her husband as he staggered to his feet. 'From now on, things are going to be different around here.'

These were fine words, but they did not pay the bills, a situation that was made worse when it became obvious to Tillie that her husband's love affair with the bottle was now too well known for him to ever be offered steady work again. Fortunately, Tillie was able to get another job and life eventually settled back to normal.

Inwardly, however, Tillie was a worried woman. She had gained the admiration and respect of the community when she had flattened her boss, and she was anxious not to revert to being the nonentity she had once been, something that would eventually happen once the memory of the episode had faded from people's minds. That is unless she came up with something new to keep attention focused on her in such a way that she would continue to be respected – even feared – in the neighbourhood. The idea she eventually conceived was staggering in its audacity. She would become a clairvoyant.

This was not so absurd as it might seem. The people

of Little Poland were mostly from peasant stock and had brought all their deep-rooted superstitions with them including the conviction that certain people had the gift of prophecy. There was only one snag to this idea. A fabulous cook Tillie might be, but a natural clairvoyant she was not.

But Tillie had already decided how she would solve that problem. She began prophesying that certain domestic pets in the neighbourhood were about to die, even telling people the day their pets would die. The fact that the poor beasts always died on schedule was hardly surprising, as Tillie always fed the animals a few tasty morsels of meat laced with poison the day before. All of a sudden, Tillie was a local celebrity again. If they did not actually cross themselves when she passed them in the street, the local people certainly regarded her with awe and were careful to treat her with great respect.

Having spent several years in killing off half the cat and dog population in the neighbourhood, Tillie began to aspire to greater things. She began to cast contemplative glances in the direction of her husband.

'John has the mark of death on him,' she announced one day to her nearest neighbour.

'It never fails to amaze me how you can tell,' the neighbour said in wonder.

'It's because of this natural gift that has been granted me,' Tillie said modestly. 'There are times, though, when I wish I didn't have it.' She glanced up at the room where her husband was sleeping off one of his hangovers, blissfully unaware of what was in store for him. 'I think he will go next Thursday.'

The evening before her husband was due to die, Tillie served him one of those thick, nourishing stews for which she was justly famous – only this time she added arsenic. The next day John Mitkiewitz passed away, dead on schedule.

When, in due course, Tillie received an unexpected cheque for a thousand dollars, it suddenly dawned on her that by sending her husband to an early grave, she had discovered a very useful way of supplementing her income.

After a suitable interval of mourning, Tillie went to see a marriage broker again. Although her looks and figure had not improved with the passing of the years, she now had the asset of having a thousand dollars in the bank. There are always men around who put money before anything else, and the marriage broker therefore was able to produce another husband for Tillie. This was John Ruskowski, a railroad worker. He lasted exactly three months before Tillie sent him to join her first husband in the All Saints cemetery.

Now better off to the extent of a further two thousand dollars' insurance money, Tillie took herself off once more to see the marriage broker, who arranged that she should meet Joseph Guszkowski, a railroad labourer who also happened to be looking for a mate. When Tillie was trundled in for his inspection, Guszkowski did not much like what he saw and was rude enough to say so in Tillie's presence. 'I wanted someone who was young and pretty,' he said indignantly.

Tillie must have felt like getting up and hitting him. Instead, much to Guszkowski's alarm, she began to cry.

Not knowing what he was in for, Guszkowski weakly agreed to move into Tillie's apartment on a trial basis. Rather surprisingly, this seemed to work out very well – at least for the first two months, when Tillie began seeing into the future again.

Tillie went through the same routine as before, which was to decide which day Joseph was to die, and then serve him up one of her delectable stews spiked with arsenic the day beforehand. On this occasion her victim had been granted only a short lease of life, as she had been mortally offended by his attitude in the marriage broker's office. In due course, Joseph Guszkowski joined the swelling number of Tillie's victims. This time there was no insurance money forthcoming. Revenge, rather than greed, had been the motive, and Tillie was not unduly concerned. What was important to her was that she had rid herself of a man she had positively disliked, leaving her free to marry again.

This time Tillie did not rush into marriage. Instead she waited for more than a year before she approached the marriage broker, who made a great show of welcoming her, as Tillie could now almost be called one of her regular customers. 'I think I may have just the man for you,' she told Tillie.

The man she had in mind was a gentle soul named Frank Kupczyk, who, strange as it may seem, took an instant liking to Tillie. As for Tillie, she was now over fifty and at an age when one would have thought that any romantic notions of falling wildly in love were long since past. Instead, when she first set eyes on Frank Kupczyk, she knew that she had met the one man she had always dreamed of meeting when she had been a young girl.

As was the custom, the newlyweds held a marriage feast to which all the neighbours and relatives were invited. Among them was Rose Chudzinski, a distant relative of the bride. Rose being a young and attractive woman, Tillie kept a wary eye on her throughout the day. It soon became obvious that Rose was not interested in Frank, but kept looking at Tillie in what can only be described as a distinctly unfriendly manner. As the party progressed well into the night, Tillie noticed that Rose kept well to herself, and spent most of the time in a corner glowering in Tillie's direction. At last, she could stand it no longer.

Lurching over to her, Tillie demanded, 'What's the matter? Why do you keep staring at me all the time?'

Rose looked at her coldly. 'I keep wondering how it is you came to lose three men in a row. I've also been wondering just how long your new husband is going to last before he joins the others in the cemetery.' With that, Rose detached herself from the wall where she had been leaning and left the party without another word, leaving Tillie standing there dumbfounded.

For the rest of that evening, Tillie's mind must have been in a turmoil. She had disposed of three men without drawing any unwelcome attention to herself. Now, just when she was in sight of spending the rest of her life with a man she truly loved, Rose had suddenly begun to voice suspicions that Tillie was a triple murderess, and was likely to repeat these suspicions to all and sundry. Surely no wedding reception was blighted to such a degree as Tillie's was that evening.

By the following morning, Tillie's mind was made up. She would have to dispose of Rose before she started making her suspicions known all over the neighbourhood.

It is perhaps interesting to examine the probable reasons why Tillie had got away with it for so long, how she had avoided being questioned by the police, or refused a death certificate by one of the doctors who had examined the corpses. After all, there had been dozens of murder cases where some astute doctor or a sharp detective had brought a far more cunning poisoner than Tillie to justice.

There had been a number of factors that had worked in Tillie's favour. She had been married to her first husband for more than twenty-five years before she had despatched him, and there was no reason why she should be suspected of murder – especially as the insurance money had only been a trifling amount, and hardly enough to murder for. On the two occasions where insurance money had been paid out, it had been done so by two different insurance companies with no connecting link. But the thing that shielded her most was her social background. Murder by poisoning has always been a middle-class activity, and one that was liable to be overlooked by an overworked doctor who was more used to dealing with gunshot or stab wounds in a community such as Little Poland, where murder resulted from a fit of temper, rather than a premeditated act. As for the police, they were too busy dealing with the flood of petty crimes that are always rife in an area where money is short to even suspect Tillie, whom they saw merely as a rather batty middle-aged woman with a local reputation for being something of a clairvoyant.

Even so, one would have thought that Tillie might have hesitated before tempting providence by killing Rose Chudzinski. On this occasion, however, she had no option but to go through with it if she were to save herself from being arrested, when a lot of unwelcome questions would be asked, and the bodies of her three victims exhumed.

The next day she hurried round to see Rose Chudzinski. We do not know what occurred between the two women, but obviously Tillie had lulled Rose's suspicions enough for her to allow Tillie to become a regular visitor. When several weeks had passed it seemed that the danger had been averted. But Tillie felt she could not let it rest at that. Rose still had to die, just in case her suspicions surfaced again. She began to speak gloomily about Rose's future.

'I'm going round to see Rose Chudzinski,' she announced to her husband one morning. 'I'm certain she is going to die tomorrow. I think I should see her before she goes. Of course, I won't say a word about her dying so soon.'

Her husband, who had complete faith in Tillie's powers of clairvoyance, nodded. 'The poor girl! Do try and make her last day as happy as possible.'

Tillie went off to see Rose and stayed long enough to make her a nice stew, having already thoughtfully visited the butcher beforehand. Before the following day was out one of Tillie's special stews had claimed another victim.

Amazingly, Tillie got away with it yet again. After that

she settled down to a normal married life with the man she loved. Her reputation for being a clairvoyant began to wane slightly, though she continued to keep her hand in by finishing off the occasional cat or dog.

Her full powers did not come into being again until 1920, when she accurately prophesied the death of three children whose parents she had quarrelled with over some trivial matter. It was a bad year for Tillie, for after five years of happily married life, her husband began to develop an interest in other women. Tillie was outraged at the thought of her beloved Frank looking at another woman, let alone contemplating what it would be like to go to bed with any of them. If her husband did not want her any more, then no one else would have him, Tillie decided. If this seems to be an overreaction to a commonplace situation, one has to remember that Tillie was now prepared to murder anybody who crossed her in any way.

When it came to it, she showed no compunction whatsoever in getting rid of the man she had once loved so dearly, and had lived with in complete harmony for the previous five years. Now she could not wait to be rid of him, such was her vengeful fury.

Within a few days, Frank Kupczyk's neighbours began to give him funny looks as he passed them in the street; Tillie's full powers as a clairvoyant had suddenly returned, and she was now putting it about that shortly she would be a widow again.

'I don't know what I have done to deserve this,' Tillie told her neighbour. 'This will make the fourth husband I have lost.'

In due course, Frank left the house as Tillie's other husbands had – via the front door in the cheapest coffin that Tillie could find.

Being a woman who never knew when she should give up, Tillie went off once again in search of a husband. The unlucky man she chose this time was Anton Klimek, an inoffensive little man who looked as if he would give her no trouble and who was happy to marry her, no doubt encouraged to commit this insane act of folly by Tillie's steadily increasing bank balance, recently swelled by an insurance payout on the life of the late Frank Kupczyk.

What put an end to this marriage was not another woman, but two dogs that Klimek had owned for a number of years. Tillie loathed dogs as much as she disliked cats. When she began to complain about the dogs, Anton Klimek had already come to realize that Tillie was impossible to live with and was therefore disposed to shrug off her complaints.

'You prefer those two dogs to me,' Tillie accused him.

'That's not true,' Anton said mildly. 'Anyway, I'm not getting rid of them just to please you.'

'We'll see about that,' Tillie said darkly.

When Anton came home one evening, it was to find the two dogs lying dead on the doormat. Appalled and grief-stricken by what he knew instinctively was her wanton killing of the two animals, he rushed from the house and went to see his brother John, who lived in a nearby street.

'What am I going to do about this woman?' Anton

asked tearfully, after he had finished telling his brother what had happened.

'There's nothing you can do now,' John told him. 'You should never have married her. A woman who has already buried four husbands . . .' His voice trailed off and he lapsed into a thoughtful silence while Anton continued to rail against Tillie's behaviour in general. 'Sometimes I think she's quite mad,' he confided to his brother, just before he left.

When Anton arrived home that evening, he found that the bodies had been removed and Tillie was busy preparing the evening meal. Surprisingly, she seemed in a good mood. 'I'm making you one of my special stews,' she called out as she stirred in the arsenic. Since Anton had gone off, she had decided that he, too, would have to go.

It is difficult to follow the workings of Tillie's deranged mind at this stage. She had rid herself of the two dogs, and at the same time made it clear to Anton that when she gave him an order, she expected it to be carried out immediately – or else. So why did she now want him dead? One only has to study the pattern of her behaviour whenever she killed to find the answer. Anyone who disagreed with her on a major issue or presented a threat to her was promptly poisoned. Anton had shown an unexpected rebellious streak in his nature, therefore he, too, had to join the rest of her victims in the local churchyard. Apart from all this, she was reaching the stage when she enjoyed killing just for the sake of it.

The person responsible for Tillie's ultimate downfall was John Klimek. After his brother's visit he had spent the whole evening pondering over the saga of Tillie's extraordinarily bad luck with her marriages, and the way she had killed Anton's dogs. After a sleepless night, he went the next morning to see the Chicago police and voiced his suspicions.

'I don't believe all this nonsense going around that my brother's wife is able to foresee her husbands' deaths,' he said. 'I think she killed them. And what's more, I have the feeling that my brother's life is now in danger.'

If it had been a busy day at the station, the police might have dismissed his story as being pure surmise and not to be taken seriously. Fortunately for Anton, they wasted no time in getting to his flat, where they found him ill in bed and in agonizing pain. A doctor was summoned, who diagnosed arsenical poisoning and was able to pull him back from the brink of death.

Tillie was arrested in the October of 1921, and the run-up to her trial was accompanied by the usual sensational headlines that made it all too clear to the shocked inhabitants of Little Poland that they had been harbouring in their midst a woman who had killed no less than eight times, to say nothing of the dozens of cats and dogs she had also killed off on the way.

At her trial Tillie gave a bravura performance in the dock as she hysterically denied the charges against her. Her general demeanour was such as to make it obvious to all that she was mentally unstable, and she was lucky enough to get away with a life sentence.

In prison she offered to cook for her fellow prisoners. Not surprisingly, the offer was refused.

ARSENIC FOR ADA

Everitt Appelgate and Mary Creighton
(USA 1936)

Everitt Appelgate and his wife Ada were an unattractive-looking couple, especially the wife, who turned the scales at over 220 lb, and was completely lacking in any charm to compensate for her excessive poundage and shapeless figure which resembled that of a Sumo wrestler when she undressed for bed. Everitt Appelgate was a blubber-lipped, doleful-looking man, as well he might be, married to Ada and living near the poverty line on his modest salary working as one of the administrators of the Nassau County Veterans Bureau. They had one child, an eleven-year-old daughter named Agnes.

Seeing this drab and unappetizing-looking couple together, the last thing you would have imagined was that one of them could become the central figure in a steamy murder case, in which sex was such a predominant factor that it became a *cause célèbre* that held the United States in thrall for the duration of the trial held in 1935, when Everitt Appelgate stood in the dock beside Mary Frances Creighton, for the murder of his wife Ada.

Mary Creighton was the wife of John Creighton, a member of the Second Division of the American Legion, of which Appelgate was Commander. The Creightons were likewise a fairly unattractive-looking couple. John was one of those stolid men who seemed half-asleep all the time, and had the look of a man who was never going to get very far in life, while Mary was an unsmiling woman who was already running to fat although she was still relatively young. They had two children, a fourteen-

year-old daughter named Ruth and an eleven-year-old
son named Jackie.

Although Everitt and John Creighton were on speaking terms, the two couples did not really become
friendly until they all met up at a dance, where Everitt
suggested that they could cut living costs by the
Appelgates moving into the Creightons' bungalow at
12 Bryant Place, in Baldwin on Long Island. As this
was in 1934, when the country was in the throes of the
Depression, when every dollar counted with chronically
hard-up families such as the Appelgates and the Creightons, John Creighton happily agreed to the suggestion –
something he most certainly would not have done if he
had known that Everitt had the morals of a buck rabbit.

The initial sleeping arrangements were settled easily
enough, with Mr and Mrs Appelgate sleeping in one of
the two bedrooms, while the Creightons occupied the
other. The two daughters shared an attic room which
could only be reached by going through the Creightons'
bedroom, while Jackie slept on the enclosed porch.

To all appearances, the two families were typical of
the lower middle-class American family units struggling
to maintain a respectable façade in the face of the
seemingly everlasting escalation in the cost of living
which always hit the lower income groups the hardest.
If the Creightons, in particular, strived to appear a
respectable family, it was for the good reason that they
had a few dark secrets they had no wish to be made
public.

In 1923 they had been put on trial for the murder of
Mary Creighton's younger brother, whose death has

been put down to arsenical poisoning. The Creightons had been acquitted, but Mary Creighton had not seen the last of a courtroom. Some time later she was arrested and accused of murdering her mother-in-law, again by using arsenic, and once again she was acquitted. Although the Creightons had been declared innocent on both these occasions, it was not the sort of subject one liked to talk about over the garden fence with a neighbour, and the Creightons had gone through life ever since dreading the day when someone might find out about their past. As it happened, someone did find out, someone, moreover, who was in the position of doing them the most harm. This was John Creighton's so-called friend, Everitt Appelgate, who kept the information to himself to use at some opportune moment, should the occasion arise.

That occasion came some months after the Appelgates had moved into their new abode. Everitt, as has already been indicated, was a one for the ladies, and, despite his unprepossessing appearance, had chalked up a fair number of conquests in that direction. He now began to cast a contemplative eye on Mary Creighton, and acquired the habit of marching through the Creightons' bedroom on the pretext of wanting to see if his daughter was nicely tucked up for the night. Neither John nor Mary took very kindly to Everitt parading across their bedroom when they were preparing to go to bed, but neither said anything as John was up for promotion in the American Legion and they had no wish to antagonize Everitt, who had the final say in the matter.

Inflamed by seeing Mary in a state of undress, Everitt decided that the time had come for him to take matters further. One day when she was in bed with a cold, and her husband and Ada were both out, he marched into her bedroom, clutching a number of pornographic pictures in his clammy hand.

'Look at these, Mary!' he exclaimed. 'I've just come across them. You might like to take a look at them.' Sitting on the edge of the bed, he watched her as she flipped through them.

'Why show me these?' she frowned. 'Do you expect them to get me going, or something? If so, you're in for a disappointment. I find them quite disgusting.'

'Don't be like that!' Everitt protested.

'What's more, I shall tell my husband.'

It was then that Everitt played his master card. 'I wouldn't do that if I were you. I might be tempted to tell Ruth how you both went on trial for murder way back in the twenties. I don't think she would be very happy, do you?'

Mary Creighton blenched. 'We were both acquitted.'

'I still think that Ruth would be very upset.'

Mary thought about it for a moment, and then pulled back the bedclothes. 'All right. You'd better get in.'

Everitt's approach could hardly be ranked as one of the great romantic seductions of all time, but for Mary the experience turned out to be a pleasurable one, after having lived all those years with her husband, who seemed to have fallen into a permanent torpor as far as sex was concerned after Jackie had been born. A whole year passed with Mary Creighton and Everitt Appelgate jumping into bed together whenever the opportunity presented itself. But by this time Mary's charms had already begun to pall with Everitt. If he did not exactly yawn when Mary summoned him to her bedroom, he did not respond with the same alacrity that he had once shown. The fizz had definitely gone from the affair as far as Everitt was concerned, and he was now looking elsewhere for his entertainment.

He found it with, of all people, Creighton's daughter Ruth, who had grown into an extremely attractive fifteen-year-old. Everitt, who seems to have been very unimaginative and crude in his approach, began to take Ruth on his rounds when he went to see the war veterans on relief, and it was on one of those occasions that he showed her a lavishly illustrated book of a pornographic nature to see what her reaction would be. Ruth's eyes glistened with interest as she turned the pages. 'It's really fun, isn't it, Uncle Ev?' she said as she returned the book to him.

Emboldened by Ruth's reaction to the book, he then took her to a school dance where he was due to operate the lights from an enclosed booth. It was while they were in the booth that Everitt took time off from his work to introduce Ruth to sex, to which she responded with considerable enthusiasm. As such opportunities as these were very rare, Everitt next came up with the outrageous suggestion that Ruth should come to his bedroom while Ada was asleep.

'But surely Auntie will see us,' Ruth said reasonably.

'Not if I give her a sleeping pill.'

From then on Ruth took to tip-toeing through her

family's room at intermittent intervals as she made her way to Uncle Everitt, who was wide awake and waiting, while Ada snored gustily beside him in a heavily drugged sleep. She never once awoke while Ruth and Everitt happily whiled away the time beside her.

Although Mary Creighton had no idea what was going on, she was only too well aware that Everitt was no longer interested in her. She noticed Ruth and Everitt exchanging meaningful glances across the table and she began to wonder, deciding to keep a close eye on the pair of them. Unfortunately for Everitt, who had become completely besotted with Ruth, he became careless in his desire to get his hands on her at every possible chance. Taking her into the garage, he was in the back of the car with her when he suddenly became aware of Mary gazing at them through the window. Ruth fled back to the house, leaving Everitt to face Mary.

'All right, Mary,' Everitt said calmly. 'What are you going to do about it? Tell your husband? I wouldn't do that if I were you.'

Mary realized that once again Everitt held the one master card that would keep her from saying a word to her husband. 'Do you love Ruth?' she asked weakly.

'If it wasn't for the fact that I'm already married, I'd marry her tomorrow,' Everitt told her.

And there the matter was left for the time being.

Some time during the beginning of September 1935, another factor was added to complicate matters still further for Everitt, who had so far managed to sidestep every obstacle that had been put in his way. This one was to present a far more serious problem for him. A near

neighbour named Mrs Olive Salket had informed Ada in
tones of incredulous horror that she had been looking
through some back numbers of a newspaper when she
read that the Creightons had been tried for murder in
1923.

'Please don't tell anyone,' the neighbour implored
her.

'I won't tell a soul,' Ada said as she went off to tell
her husband.

When Ada broke the news, Everitt's doleful-looking
face took on the expression of a man who has just
received a death sentence. Knowing his wife, he realized
the news would be all round the whole neighbourhood
in no time at all, and the Creightons would be forced to
leave the district. Later that day he broke the news to
Mary, who thought about it for some moments. 'We
don't want that to happen, do we?' she said finally.

Everitt knew exactly what that look meant. In exchange for Mary keeping the matter from her husband
for as long as possible, she would expect them to resume
their relationship. Everitt cleared his throat. 'I've been
thinking, Mary, that it might be a good idea if we got our
relationship back on its old footing.'

'Why not?' Mary said. 'In the meantime I'd better go
and see this woman who is trying to ruin our lives. After
all, we were declared innocent at the trial.'

'I'd rather you didn't,' Everitt said. 'If Ada learns I've
been talking to you about this, she won't be very
pleased.'

From then on, Everitt found himself in the unusual
position of having an affair with both the mother and

daughter, a situation which he must have found somewhat nerve-racking, trying to satisfy the two of them in
a small bungalow where there could have been little
privacy amongst seven occupants. If his behaviour
seems outrageous, Everitt was to cap it when he decided
that his wife was an encumbrance he could well do
without – a decision that no doubt would have been
helped along by the fact that Ada Appelgate now
weighed an elephantine 270 lb. This problem he hoped
shortly to resolve by feeding her arsenic in her food.

What follows borders on the incredible. Surmising
that Mary Creighton had had some experience in these
matters, he asked her to help him send Ada on her way,
and Mary agreed – for no other reason, it seems, than
that she was in fear of Everitt exposing her affair with
him to her husband.

One would be justified in thinking that this was hardly
a motive for helping to kill another human being, but
having already murdered two people, Mary had come to
see poisoning people as the solution to a number of life's
little problems. It never seems to have occurred to her
that it might have been more to the point if she had
removed Everitt by the same means, rather than Ada,
thereby permanently ridding herself of someone who
posed such a threat to her. Nor does it seem to have
occurred to her that having already murdered two
people, it was asking a little too much to hope to get
away with it for a third time.

The seeds of the undoing of this unholy pair had
already been sown before they agreed to poison Ada.
Against Everitt's wishes, Mary Creighton had been

unwise enough to visit Mrs Salket, and in the course of conversation Mary had told her that her brother had committed suicide by poisoning himself with arsenic because he was dying of cancer.

'I didn't tell the court the truth when we were unjustly accused of his murder, otherwise the insurance company wouldn't have paid out,' Mary told her.

'Who got the insurance money?' Mrs Salket asked pointedly.

Mary hesitated. 'We did. It was my brother's dearest wish that we should have it.'

Having got Mary's agreement to help to carry out the murder, Everitt took her to the local drug store, where she spotted exactly what he wanted – a rodent killer called 'Rough on Rats'. 'That's the stuff I used on my brother,' she whispered. 'You can't go wrong with that. What's more, you don't have to sign the register for it.'

On 13th September, Mrs Appelgate suddenly complained of feeling unwell and took to her bed. The doctor, who was already treating her for her weight problem, was called out, and as she seemed to be in a serious condition, ordered her to be moved to the hospital, much to Everitt's chagrin, as he had been planning to kill her off with a series of small doses of arsenic which he hoped would make her subsequent death less obvious. Not surprisingly, once she was free of the pair's deadly attentions, Ada recovered rapidly and was back home within a few days.

The next time round, Everitt and Mary saw to it that Ada died quickly, and by 27th September she was dead.

The doctor was summoned, and after examining the body, decided that Ada's death had been brought about by her excess weight putting a strain on the heart. He issued a death certificate in which the cause of death was put down to coronary occlusion.

Everitt and Mary might have got away with it if Mrs Salket hadn't still been convinced that the Creightons had been guilty of murder and hadn't started voicing her opinions to her closest neighbours. This being small-town America, where rumours tended to travel fast, it was not long before Mary heard about it. She guessed at once the source of the story going around. In a towering rage she retired to the kitchen, where she baked a cake in which arsenic was one of the ingredients. When it was done she took a slice around to Mrs Salket.

'This is made from a secret recipe of mine,' she said. 'I thought you might like to try it.'

As it happened, Mary must have put insufficient arsenic in the cake as Mrs Salket ate some of it, complaining that it tasted a little bitter, and threw the rest of it away. The next day she was taken violently ill, but not ill enough to die. When she recovered she went to see Mary Creighton.

'I believe you tried to poison me,' she accused her. 'I'm sure you put arsenic in that piece of cake you brought over.'

Mary regarded her calmly. 'That's a downright lie. Moreover, if I hear that you've been spreading that story around, I shall sue you for slander. You'll find then that spreading lies like that will cost you a great deal of money.'

But Mrs Salket was not so easily cowed into silence.
Storming angrily out of the house she went home and
wrote a letter to Martin Littleton, the District Attorney,
telling him all she knew about the Creightons and the
Appelgates, and of Mary's attempt to poison her after
she became aware that Mary had murdered Ada Appelgate. Normally the District Attorney would have dismissed it as another of those crackpot letters he was
always receiving. But the name Appelgate struck a
chord, and he suddenly remembered Appelgate coming
into his office and handing him a number of anonymous
and abusive letters he had received, in which Appelgate
had been referred to as a lecher who was a menace to the
community, and his wife a loud-mouthed liar. Fortunately, Mrs Salket had given the date of the Creightons'
trial and he was easily able to check up on the case. After
reading the accounts of the trial, he called in Harold H.
King, Chief of the Nassau County Detectives, and
showed him Mrs Salket's letter.

'I want this checked out. For one thing, see if an
autopsy was carried out on Mrs Appelgate.'

Inspector King wasted no time in going to see the
doctor who had attended Ada. 'Bearing in mind the
condition of my patient, there was no reason to think she
had died of anything else but a coronary occlusion,' the
doctor said. 'But now you've brought up this matter, I
was rather surprised that she became ill again so soon
after her discharge from hospital.'

'Was an autopsy carried out?'

The doctor looked embarrassed. 'I didn't think at the
time that it was necessary.'

King reported back to the District Attorney, who immediately ordered that the Creightons and Everitt Appelgate be asked to attend his office for questioning. 'It'll be interesting to see Appelgate's reaction when we ask him to sign the form, giving us permission to carry out the autopsy,' he said.

As soon as he met John Creighton, Littleton was certain that he knew nothing about Ada's death. He did not feel the same way about Everitt Appelgate and Mary Creighton, although their answers to all the questions he put to them were convincing enough. Even when he brought up the matter of Mrs Salket's accusation that she had tried to poison her, Mary had given a glib answer.

'I'm a rotten cake-maker, so I'm not surprised she didn't like it,' Mary said wryly. 'But as to accusing me of trying to poison her, that's utter nonsense. But then, she's always disliked me.'

What worried Littleton was the way both of them were at great pains to support the other's statement, which made him suspect that they had been partners in the possible crime he was investigating. The answer, of course, lay in the results of the autopsy.

Before they left the District Attorney asked them to sign their statements. After they had gone he began to wonder about the anonymous letters that Appelgate had received. They were obviously not from Mrs Salket as her handwriting did not match that in the anonymous letters. He then wondered if they had been written by Everitt Appelgate to himself in order to give the police the impression that the Appelgates had an enemy in the town, and thus divert suspicion from himself when it came to murdering his wife. As a matter of routine, he then compared the signatures on the letters with Mary Creighton's signature on her statement. To his surprise, they matched.

Littleton asked to see Mary alone this time when he confronted her with the matching signatures. Instead of trying to deny she had written the letters, Mary readily confessed they had been from her. 'I wanted the Appelgates out of the house,' she explained. 'Especially *him*. He was always making passes at me, and he was a very bad influence on my daughter.'

Littleton looked at the dates and saw that the letters had been written months before Ada had died. 'What good did you think they might do?' he asked.

'Well, I knew it was no good speaking to my husband about Everitt. He's too soft-hearted, so I thought if I made trouble for Everitt, and the police started investigating him, he might move.'

Littleton let it go at that for the time being and sat back to await the results of the autopsy, something which Everitt was now trying to prevent by speaking in the right quarters of the American Legion.

'If Littleton persists in trying to go through with the autopsy, I'll see the Attorney General and have him thrown out of office,' Everitt told some of his friends in the Legion.

It was the worst thing he could have done. Needless to say, no one made any attempt to stop the District Attorney, though certain members of the Legion who had no great liking for Everitt made sure that the District Attorney's office was made aware of what he was trying to do.

Littleton's reaction was to say nothing and sit back and wait with the growing certainty in his own mind that the autopsy was going to show that Ada Appelgate had died of arsenical poisoning. Ada's body was exhumed at night and her organs taken away by a Dr Gertler, who found they contained 3.7 grains of arsenic, more than enough to kill a large animal, let alone Ada.

Everitt and the Creightons were called to the office of the District Attorney the same night and informed of the coroner's findings. Everitt and Mary were then taken into separate rooms, where they both made a statement in which each tried to put most of the blame on the other.

Mary claimed that on the day of the murder Everitt had handed her a packet of white powder and had told her to mix the contents in Ada's milk. 'Everything I did was because I was frightened of him,' Mary said. 'You know that from when you questioned me about the letters I wrote.'

'What about the attempt to murder Olive Salket?' Littleton asked her.

'I did put a pinch or two of rat poison in the cake,' she admitted. 'But she deserved it.'

Everitt told a rather different story. While admitting that he was involved in the murder, he claimed that Mary had administered the poison.

'Was Mrs Creighton ever your mistress?' he was asked.

'Of course not,' Everitt said indignantly. 'She was far too old.'

When Mary was informed of Everitt's remark, her face was a sight to see. 'He's a liar!' she shouted. 'I was good enough for him until he started something with my daughter.'

'Tell me more,' Littleton murmured.

Mary was only too willing to oblige. Her enthralled audience listened in silence while Mary told them the whole sordid story of Everitt's infatuation with her fifteen-year-old daughter, and how Everitt had planned to kill his wife for her, while at the same time trying to show herself as his unwilling accomplice.

'And that's it?' Littleton enquired, when she had finished.

Mary nodded silently, beginning to realize too late that she had already said too much. Later, she was to make a third statement running to some thirty pages, which was so full of obvious half truths and downright lies that it only made her case worse for the lawyer who was to defend her.

Mary Creighton and Everitt Appelgate were charged with murder, and went on trial on 15th January 1936, with Judge Courtland H. Johnson presiding over the case. The result of the trial was a foregone conclusion from the start, and on 30th January they were both found guilty and sentenced to die in the electric chair on 9th March. American law being what it is, all number of futile appeals were lodged before the executions took place on 16th July, in the notorious Sing Sing prison. Everitt walked stoically to his death, but Mary Creighton had become so paralysed with fear over the few days prior to her execution that she was unable to walk. With the same lack of humanity she had shown Ada Appelgate, she was briskly bundled into a wheelchair and trundled to the death chamber, where she was executed in a semi-conscious condition.

QUEEN VICTORIA WISHED HER DEAD

Mrs Florence Maybrick (1889)

In 1917, an ageing American woman of 55, named Mrs Florence Chandler, arrived in the tiny hamlet of South Kent in Connecticut, where she was to spend the rest of her life in merciful obscurity. She had suffered much in life, and there had been a time when she had had a substantial amount of money in the bank, but this had dwindled down to $2,000, and it was for this reason that she had come to the area to take a job as housekeeper to Henrietta Banwell, the owner of a chicken farm. It was not long before Mrs Banwell and her employee ran into that age-old problem that sometimes exists between employer and employee; Henrietta wanted value for money, while her employee, who had been used to having servants herself, didn't want to do any work at all. Out on the street before she had hardly settled in, Mrs Chandler rented a flat in town while she had a modest three-bedroomed cottage built for herself on a plot of land on the fringe of town.

Generally speaking, Americans are friendly, outgoing people, and it was only natural that her new neighbours should want to know all they could about the newcomer in their midst, who was obviously a lady of refinement from the way she spoke, but had come down in the world. But Mrs Chandler would have none of it. She was quite willing to pass the time of day in small talk, but when questions began to be asked about her past private life, she spoke in evasive terms from which one could only gather that her husband and family were all dead. When it became obvious that she would be far happier left alone, people respected her wishes while remaining on friendly terms.

As the years went by, Mrs Chandler grew pro-
gressively more eccentric, and so poor that she raided
her neighbours' dustbins for newspapers which she
loved to read but was too proud to ask for them to be
passed on to her. As she wandered from dustbin to
dustbin, with a sack in which to put the papers, she
began to resemble one of those pathetic bag ladies one
sees in London or New York, carrying their worldly
possessions in paper bags and parcels.

Despite seeming to be such a lonely figure with only
her memories for company, which she would have
preferred to forget anyway, Mrs Chandler was very far
from being alone since she had begun to acquire her
cats, which she had collected around her by taking in all
the strays in the neighbourhood. The cats became her
only reason for living, and she devoted most of her
waking hours to feeding and looking after them. Seeing
that Mrs Chandler was living on scraps of food herself,
a kindly couple named Austin delivered her baskets of
food whenever they could, although they knew that she
must have other benefactors who helped to keep her and
her cats alive. There was, for instance, the man who
came in a car once a month and handed her an envelope
and then drove off. Inevitably, this led to a great deal of
speculation about Mrs Chandler's background, all of it
wide of the mark.

Like most lonely eccentrics, Mrs Chandler easily took
offence and often quarrelled with people over some
fancied insult. She even quarrelled with the Austins, but
not before she had given Mrs Austin a black Spanish
dress trimmed with lace, in gratitude for all they had

done for her. With the dress had come a coat hanger that Mrs Chandler must have forgotten to remove, for it bore her real name – a name, moreover, which made the Austins realize why she had been so secretive about her past. The Austins, being thoroughly decent people, decided to keep silent, which they did until Mrs Chandler eventually died.

In the last years of her life she became something of a trial to her neighbours when she began wandering into their houses unannounced, much to the consternation of the occupants when they suddenly found themselves confronted by an apparition dressed in layers of old sweaters and a blanket tied together with string and safety pins. Her neighbours must have been remarkably forbearing. Instead of getting together and trying to have her put in an institution, where she would probably have been better off, they took her meals, trying not to be ill as they entered the cottage and were immediately assailed by the horrendous smell of the filth and decay in which Mrs Chandler lived.

What disturbed her neighbours most was when she decided to kill her cats – all thirty of them – and poisoned them with arsenic, a poison with which she was not unacquainted. Some writers have put this down as an example of her irrational behaviour during the last period of her life. It is more likely that it was considered an act of mercy by a woman who was able to see through the fog of senile dementia to the time when she would die, when her cats would be at the mercy of strangers.

The end came on 23rd October 1941, when she was discovered lying dead on her bed by the milkman. 'The

Old Woman of the Woods', as she had become known, was buried two days later in the grounds of South Kent School, to whom she had bequeathed her cottage, now little more than a broken-down old shack. Among her pitiful effects had been found a family bible, two rosaries, a number of old and fading photographs, and, of course, her will. When its contents were made known, the local people learned that the wizened old lady they had known as Mrs Chandler had been the once notorious Mrs Florence Maybrick, who had been found guilty of poisoning her husband in 1889. Her sentence had caused an uproar at the time, and is an appalling example of how justice can be notably absent in an English court of law from time to time.

The story of Mrs Maybrick's downward spiral from grace to the time she stood in the dock, accused of murder, can be said to have begun when she was travelling from New York to Liverpool on the *Baltic* with her mother. She was only seventeen at the time, and could look forward to a comfortable and happy life now that she had just met and promised to marry James Maybrick, a Liverpool man more than twice her age.

Born in Mobile in Alabama in 1862, during the American Civil War, she was the daughter of a lawyer and businessman who had died in mysterious circumstances. Because it was known that her mother was being unfaithful to her husband at the time of his death, and being a hated Northerner, the rumour began to get around that she had poisoned her husband. Unperturbed by it all, her mother had calmly moved to Macon in Georgia, with her two children, a son named Holbrook, and Florence. There she had married her lover, Captain Du Barry, who was later invalided out of the army and was dead within the year.

For a woman who had spent at least part of her life in the South, where good manners and a strict observance of the rules of society are placed high on the list of priorities, Mrs Du Barry does not seem to have behaved with a great deal of discretion. After racketing around Europe and the United States, having the occasional love affair on the way, she settled in Paris, where she met and married Baron Adolph von Roques.

Her marriage gave her a title, but very little else. A Prussian officer with no morals whatsoever, Adolph systematically went through her money, while being consistently unfaithful to his wife. When drunk he physically assaulted her, and when sober enlisted her aid in a series of frauds that did nothing for her reputation, and even less for the marriage, which ended abruptly when he abandoned her in 1879.

Being a resilient woman, the Baroness packed her son off to a medical school in Paris, and then began a nomadic existence with her daughter in tow, frequently dumping her in an institution while she pursued a wild and erratic career as an unscrupulous adventuress, leaving a pile of bills in her wake each time she moved on. When she boarded the ship bound for Liverpool, accompanied by her daughter, the Baroness was running out of money, and her looks, which had been such an asset to her in the past, were beginning to fade. Hearing that Florence's shipboard friendship with Maybrick had suddenly burgeoned into an impending love match, she was slightly miffed that he had chosen Florence instead of her, but gave the girl her approval, contenting herself with the thought that a wealthy son-in-law would not be without his uses.

As for Florence, she had seen something of her mother's life style and did not wish to make the same mistakes, wanting only a secure and sheltered life which she knew she could have if she married Maybrick.

Unfortunately, both the Baroness and Florence had backed the wrong horse in Maybrick. He was forty when he married Florence. He had never been married before, but he did have a mistress in Liverpool, who had borne him five children, all of whom had died in early childhood. Although he was careful to show himself as a kind and courteous lover, he was by nature a morose and often ill-tempered man. To make matters worse for his new wife, he was an arsenic eater, a vice common to many Victorians who could afford to take it. One way and another, it was not a sound foundation on which to build a marriage.

Florence and James Maybrick were married in 1881 in St James's Church, Piccadilly, London, and the first three years of their life together were spent in the cotton state of Virginia, before they finally settled in Battle-crease House, a large and solidly built mansion in Aigburth, one of the more wealthy suburbs of Liverpool.

Outwardly, their marriage was a successful one. They had two nice children, a boy named James, and a girl they had named Gladys. They lived well and had a busy social life, attending balls and civic functions when they were not entertaining at home or being entertained by friends, when most of the evenings were devoted to playing cards or talking business. It was a rather shallow existence, but no worse than that led by many others in the Liverpool world of commerce, where an ostentatious display of wealth on social occasions was considered far more important than displaying a knowledge of the arts. The only event that marred Florence's carefree existence at that time was when she learned that her brother Holbrook had died of consumption in Paris.

But all this entertaining and junketing around Liverpool was beginning to put a strain on Maybrick's resources. In an attempt to economize, he tried to curb Florence's careless expenditure on the housekeeping, something she strongly resented, having always been given her head until then. They had already quarrelled over his habitual arsenic eating. He often ingested it as much as three times a day until he was now dependent on it. As he confessed on one occasion, to a friend, 'arsenic is meat and drink to me. I take it when I can get it, but the doctors won't put any in medicine except now and then; that only tantalizes me.'

Now they began to quarrel loudly and often over the housekeeping and the money Florence spent on her wardrobe, which she argued was essential if they were to keep up appearances. To make matters even worse at home, Florence learned that her husband had been going with other women. Instead of behaving like most Victorian women, who turned a blind eye to their husbands' infidelities, Florence's reaction was to have a few lovers herself, including her brother-in-law, Edwin, and Alfred Brierley, a cotton broker who was on good terms with her husband.

By then, whatever love that had existed between herself and her husband was gone. For Florence, James Maybrick was now only someone who paid the bills and kept her short of money, while happily squandering it on other women. For his part, Maybrick no longer treated his wife with the same loving care and consideration he had shown her until quite recently. Now he saw her merely as the mother of his children and someone who still had her uses at the dinner table, where she played the role of the gracious hostess to his guests. In this she was no different to many other Victorian women who were trapped in an unhappy marriage, where the husband held the purse strings and the wife was a prisoner because she had no money of her own. The only difference with Florence was that she thought she had found a way out of this sort of trap because of Brierley, whom she was convinced would marry her, given a little encouragement.

With this in mind, Florence told her husband that she was going to London on a shopping expedition, booked a suite in a London hotel, and was later joined there by Brierley. As the hotel was Flatman's in Henrietta Street, a favourite with the northern cotton men, she must have known she was courting trouble. To compound this seeming act of folly, she had booked the rooms in the name of Mr and Mrs Maybrick. The weekend passed off without incident, and she returned home more convinced than ever that Brierley was her passport to a happier life than the one she had at the moment.

One of the very few things that Florence and James Maybrick did enjoy together was going to the races, and towards the end of March they went to Aintree to watch the Grand National, which was celebrating its fiftieth birthday and was being attended by the Prince of Wales to celebrate the occasion. Unfortunately, Brierley was also there, and after the race he took Florence along to see the royal party without bothering to ask Maybrick's permission. Trivial as the incident was, it was one more link in the chain of events that were to lead Florence Maybrick to the very edge of the gallows.

When Florence and her husband arrived home there was a violent quarrel during which Maybrick lost his temper completely and physically attacked her, tearing her dress and giving her a black eye. Florence ran screaming into the hallway where she shouted to Miss Yapp, the children's nanny, to call a cab. Instead, Miss Yapp persuaded her to stay for the sake of the children, and made up a bed for her in one of the spare bedrooms. In the trial that was to follow not long afterwards, Miss Yapp was to be a key witness for the prosecution.

The next morning, Florence was still determined to leave Maybrick, and she went to see Dr Hopper, the family physician, to whom she complained bitterly of her husband's conduct, before going on to see a solicitor to arrange separation. After Florence had gone, Dr Hopper mulled over the situation that now existed at Battlecrease House, and then went around to see if there was anything he could do to salvage the marriage. Thanks to his intervention, Florence and her husband were reconciled, with Maybrick even stating that he would pay off Florence's debts that now amounted to £600, a not inconsiderable sum, bearing in mind that Maybrick's total income annually was in the region of £1,009.

Despite the gesture on Maybrick's part, Florence still had no intention of staying with him, and at the first opportunity she went to see Brierley, only to find that he was somewhat less than enthusiastic about the idea of marrying her.

'An affair is one thing,' he said gently. 'Marriage is quite a different matter. Maybrick is well known in these parts, and the scandal would do me immeasurable harm.'

Nothing was more clear than that, but Florence still could not accept that Brierley wanted to end their relationship. She went away convinced that Maybrick was the only reason for his reluctance to marry her.

Two weeks later, Maybrick went to London to see his elder brother, Michael, and to pay off some of the bills that Florence had run up. While he was with Michael, his brother told him that he was not looking at all well, and sent him to see his physician, Dr Charles Fuller, who examined Maybrick and found nothing seriously wrong with him, although his patient claimed he was suffering from pains in the head and a general numbness in the limbs. There was nothing sinister in this, as Maybrick was a hypochondriac, and always complaining of something, and he had a medicine cupboard stuffed with all number of patent medicines which he was always raiding. As one of his American acquaintances had once remarked, 'Maybrick has a dozen drug stores in his stomach.'

Maybrick returned to Battlecrease House and things went on very much as before, though Florence was still secretly pining for Brierley, who was keeping well out of the way, and was even planning to make a seven-week cruise around the Mediterranean in an attempt to put as much distance as possible between himself and Florence. Unwisely, as it turned out, he wrote to Florence, telling her of his intention.

On 25th April, Maybrick drew up a new will, leaving everything to the two children, and virtually cutting Florence off without a penny, with the exception of a couple of insurance policies. As for Battlecrease House and its contents, Florence was allowed to stay for 'so long as she remained a widow'. With this new will, Maybrick made it all too clear that he had not forgotten or forgiven Florence for attempting to leave him.

The date that the new will was drawn up was not without significance as it was about this time that Florence made a visit to a chemist, where she bought two dozen arsenical fly-papers.

Two days later Maybrick had an attack of vomiting and again complained that his legs felt numb. It is difficult to assess just how seriously ill he was at this time, as he still managed to attend the Wirral races. When he came home from the races he complained that he had caught a chill and immediately went to bed, telling Florence that he was suffering from pains in his chest and heart. Convinced that all the doctors were fools, including his own doctor, Maybrick wrote to his brother Michael, instructing him that if he died a postmortem was to be carried out. This sounds very much like the morbid forebodings of a hypochondriac who was convinced that he was about to die. Others might say he wrote the letter because he suspected that he was being poisoned.

If Florence was indeed attempting to poison her husband, she seems to have behaved with remarkable stupidity. Instead of allowing matters to take their course, she wrote to Brierley and gave the letter to Miss Yapp to post. Miss Yapp conveniently dropped the letter in the mud, with the intention of posting it in a new envelope – after she had read it. She had never liked her mistress, and the contents of the letter sent her scurrying back to show it to Edwin Maybrick. Edwin was equally startled by its contents and immediately wired his brother Michael, asking him to come to Battlecrease House immediately. By then Florence had bought another two dozen fly-papers from a different chemist – less than a week after her first purchase. When Michael arrived and read the letter, he immediately ordered a round-the-clock guard on his brother.

What was there in Florence's letter that caused alarm bells to ring in the minds of all those who had read it? For one thing, Florence had told Brierley there was no longer any need for him to go abroad on Maybrick's account as she was now convinced that he knew nothing of their relationship. More significantly, she had informed him that Maybrick was now *sick unto death*.

As far as the doctors were concerned, Maybrick was still very far from being on his deathbed – that is unless Florence Maybrick knew something they didn't, such as the fact that their patient was being systematically fed with poison. The general tone of the letter also made it clear that she was madly in love with Brierley, thereby giving her a motive for getting rid of her husband.

Convinced that Florence was a potential murderess, the two brothers, assisted by Miss Yapp and the two nurses who had been called in, watched Florence's every move whenever she went into the sick room. Their vigilance was rewarded when the night nurse, feigning sleep, saw Florence glide into the room and remove a bottle of meat essence and then take it to her room, only to return with it a few minutes later and replace it on the bedside table. The nurse took it away and gave it to Michael, who had it analysed. It was found to contain half a grain of arsenic. On another occasion Michael pounced on Florence changing medicine from one bottle to another. 'How dare you tamper with my brother's medicine,' he shouted. 'The only ones who are allowed to touch those bottles are myself, my brother and the two nurses.'

Despite all the family's attempts to protect Maybrick, he grew steadily worse, and on the evening of 11th May died, after kissing his two children goodbye.

On the surface of it, the case against Florence Maybrick was overwhelming. She had bought four dozen arsenical fly-papers, she had virtually been cut out of Maybrick's will, which she must have greatly resented, and she was in love with a man she was convinced would marry her, given the opportunity. Furthermore, she had been caught tampering with the bottle at Maybrick's bedside table. People have been hanged on less evidence.

Following Maybrick's death, Florence found herself surrounded by people who now obviously loathed her. Alice Yapp went out of her way to find further incriminating evidence against her, and found it in a packet of white powder labelled 'Arsenic: Cat Poison', which she had discovered in a trunk in Florence's bedroom. The nurses treated her with open contempt, as did most of the servants, while Michael made no secret of the fact that he blamed her for causing her husband's death through neglect, though never going so far as to accuse her of murder in public. Only Edwin seems to have left her alone, remembering perhaps that they were once lovers.

While Florence was out, Michael made a thorough search of the house with the over-zealous Miss Yapp at his heels. They found letters from Brierley and other men she had been with, including Edwin, who had to face his brother's wrath once he had become aware that James Maybrick had been betrayed by his younger brother.

In his determination that Florence should be brought to book for the murder of her husband, Michael had contested the doctor's verdict that his brother had died from a severe attack of gastro-enteritis, saying that he suspected arsenical poisoning and demanding a post-mortem. This was carried out on 13th May, when a minute portion of arsenic was found in the body. As James Maybrick had been stuffing himself with arsenic for years, this was hardly surprising.

Although the amount of arsenic found in the body was not enough to kill a mouse, let alone Maybrick, Michael was still convinced that Florence had poisoned his brother, and from then on kept her a prisoner in her room, refusing to allow her to see any visitors. He did, however, allow her to write to her mother, and even wrote to the Baroness himself, asking her to come at once as her daughter was in trouble. He then placed the matter in the hands of the police.

The Baroness, who had come to roost in Paris, wasted no time in answering Florence's call for help. She arrived like a ship with a full head of steam on and with all guns firing. Michael being away, the first person she saw was Edwin.

'Where is my daughter?' she demanded.

'She's in her room, but you cannot see her at the moment. The police are interviewing her.'

'The police!' the Baroness said, her voice rising. 'The police! What has been happening here exactly?'

She listened aghast to what Edwin had to say and then pushed him impatiently aside and stormed upstairs, where she found two policemen standing outside her daughter's bedroom door. Ignoring them, the Baroness barged into the room, only to find another policeman and a nurse at her daughter's bedside. Ignoring them, the Baroness bombarded her daughter with questions until she had reduced Florence to a state of hysterics. The nurse tried to intervene, only to be silenced by the Baroness.

'I know more about nursing than you do,' she told her inaccurately. 'Let me hold her hand and speak to her and she will be calm.'

'I'm in charge here,' the nurse said sharply. 'One

more word from you and I'll have you put out.'

'Better death than such dishonour,' the Baroness said in ringing tones, making an exit from the room in a manner worthy of the great Sarah Bernhardt, whom she had probably seen playing in Paris with the *Comédie Française*. When she returned to the house the following day, it was to find that the police had decided that they had a case against Florence Maybrick, who had been put under arrest and taken to Walton Gaol on the outskirts of Liverpool.

The trial of Florence Maybrick for the murder of her husband took place in St George's Hall, Liverpool, at the Summer Assizes of 1889. Florence's solicitor had obtained for her the services of Sir Charles Russell, QC, considered to be one of the best advocates of his day. His services had been obtained only with the greatest difficulty, as Sir Charles' reputation was such that he could command high fees. The Baroness raised some of the money, but most of it had been supplied by, of all people, the surviving Maybrick brothers, who had put her in the dock, but still wished that she should be given a fair trial. Brierley also supplied several hundred pounds towards her defence.

In support of Russell they had obtained William Pickford as Junior Counsel, a more than able defence lawyer. Together they made a formidable team against the case for the Crown, led by John Addison, who had none of the experience of Russell in the courtroom. Despite the seemingly overwhelming evidence against Florence, the few who believed in her innocence began to think that with Russell leading the defence she had a chance, after all, of an acquittal. They had not reckoned with Mr Justice Stephen, who was to take an almost vindictive pleasure in pronouncing the death sentence on Florence Maybrick.

If Judge Jeffries had been a hanging judge, who handed out death sentences at the slightest whiff of treason, Stephen was liable to be very hard on an accused person if they had committed adultery. Florence could therefore expect no mercy from him if the evidence pointed in the direction of her being guilty of murder. Even worse, when Justice Stephen stepped into the courtroom that morning, he was on the verge of insanity, and was to be committed to a lunatic asylum not long afterwards.

The trial lasted for seven days, and most of it was taken up by the Crown trying to establish three points: first, that Florence Maybrick was having an adulterous relationship with Brierley and was head over heels in love with him, second, that James Maybrick had died from arsenical poisoning, and, third, that the arsenic had been administered by Florence, and that she had obtained it from the arsenical fly-papers.

Her adulterous relationship with Brierley was easily established by the staff of Flatman's Hotel, nor was any attempt made to deny it by the defence. That he was poisoned by arsenic was never proven, or that Florence had knowingly administered it with the intent of killing her husband.

As for Mrs Maybrick's two purchases of the arsenical fly-papers, she maintained in a statement she made to the court towards the end of the trial that she had

obtained them to extract the arsenic from the fly-papers
in order to make up a facial lotion for her skin. As many
women in those days used arsenic for their complexions,
her explanation seemed reasonable enough – especially
as she could prove that a Dr Gregg of Brooklyn had
prescribed for her a special lotion which had contained
arsenic, but which she had subsequently lost or mislaid.
Moreover, when she had put the fly-papers to soak, she
had made no attempt to conceal what she was doing
from the servants.

In her statement to the court, Florence referred to the
bottle of meat essence and admitted that she had put
arsenic in it, but only after Maybrick had implored her
to do so, and had assured her it was quite safe. As
Maybrick was no longer around to support her statement, the jury remained unimpressed, as they had done
whenever any evidence was brought up in her favour.
Like the newspapers and most other people, the jury had
already tried her and found her guilty before they had
even entered the courtroom. In the face of a hostile judge
and jury, the defence could do little but battle on and
hope that in the end justice would prevail.

When the time came for the final speech for the
defence, Sir Charles Russell rose to his feet, knowing
that what little chance he had had in the beginning had
been destroyed when Florence had admitted putting
arsenic in the meat essence. He did not try and play
down his client's illicit relationship with Brierley, but
concentrated mostly on the manner of Maybrick's death,
maintaining that he had not died of arsenical poisoning,
but from gastro-enteritis, the symptoms of which were

almost identical to those of someone who had been poisoned by arsenic. When Sir Charles sat down at the end of his speech, he had faced too many battles in the courtroom for him not to know that he had failed to convince the jury of his client's innocence – a fact that was to haunt him for the rest of his life.

When Addison rose to make his final speech for the Crown, he knew that he had to override two awkward points if he were to obtain a verdict of guilty from the jury. There was the undeniable fact that Maybrick had been a habitual arsenic eater, and that he was also a hypochondriac who was forever taking all forms of drugs whose constant use could have caused gastro-enteritis. Addison briskly dealt with these two points by reminding the jury that Maybrick had been a healthy man until Brierley had come on the scene. If Mrs Maybrick were innocent, as she claimed, was it not a remarkable coincidence, Addison asked, that she had bought the arsenical fly-papers twice, once when Brier-ley became Florence's lover, when Maybrick was taken ill, and again when he seemed to be getting better? It was a telling point.

It is always expected that a prosecutor should use every means at his disposal to obtain a conviction, and it was therefore only natural that Addison should refer to Maybrick's death as murder carried out against a background of 'profligacy and adultery', two deliber-ately chosen, highly emotive words in the Victorian world, where any mention of moral laxity was guaran-teed to get a shocked reaction from a public that professed to have high moral principles. It is interesting to note in passing that only thirty years before this trial some of the most popular paintings at the Royal Academy were a series of three oils by Augustus Egg, titled *Past and Present*, showing the dire consequences of a wife's infidelity, which does much to explain the moral censure that was levelled against Mrs Maybrick at the time.

Mr Justice Stephen's summing up began on the sixth day of the trial, and to begin with he seemed his usual rational self, carefully examining the points that had been brought up by both the prosecution and the defence. At the end of the day his summing up had been fair and just, and slightly in favour of Mrs Maybrick, who began to believe that it would not be long before she was delivered from her ordeal.

Overnight he seems to have suffered from some sort of brainstorm. Before a packed courtroom, Mr Justice Stephen then proceeded to launch a vicious attack on Mrs Maybrick's lack of morals, which he seemed to see as being almost akin to murder. Getting into his stride, he railed against the two lovers, one who now stood in the dock weeping, while the other sat cowering in misery in the courtroom. Within minutes, a court of justice had been turned into a place where morals had become the issue, rather than murder.

Those in the courtroom who had any legal knowledge were staggered by the judge's indefensible attack, and were convinced that in view of the obvious unfairness of the summing up, the jury would go against the judge and find Mrs Maybrick not guilty.

The members of the jury, however, were all from

modest walks of life, and imbued with an awe of authority. They accepted without question Mr Justice Stephen's direction and returned to the court within thirty-five minutes with a verdict of guilty.

After sentence of death had been passed, Mrs Maybrick reeled in the dock and clutched at the handrail in front of her for support. Recovering herself almost immediately, she brushed aside the helping hands of her wardresses and walked unaided to the cell that awaited below. It was as if in those few moments she had summoned a hidden reserve of strength unknown even to herself.

At that point something rather extraordinary happened. Until that last day in court, public feeling had been against Mrs Maybrick. Now, with that characteristic sympathy for the underdog, combined with the awareness that less than justice had been done, public opinion immediately swung around in her favour. Mr Justice Stephen's carriage was pursued by a hostile crowd which had to be broken up by the police, while Mrs Maybrick's prison van, bearing her to the condemned cell, was greeted by cheers of encouragement as it passed.

The subsequent uproar which swept across this country and America, plus the best part of half a million signatures asking for a reprieve that had been handed in to the Home Secretary, put the government in an embarrassing position. To have tried to ignore all the fuss that had been caused by the results of the trial would have led to the government's downfall in the next election. As a result, the death sentence was commuted to one of life imprisonment.

One person who was definitely displeased by the decision was Queen Victoria, who thought that Mrs Maybrick should have been hanged. 'The sentence must never be further commuted,' she wrote angrily to the Home Secretary. Having already incurred her displeasure, the Home Secretary was careful not to compound the 'error' by releasing Mrs Maybrick early. She served over fourteen years before she was released on parole, despite all the enormous efforts made by many to get her released earlier. Among those who fought for her release was Sir Charles Russell, who visited her in prison just before his death.

Florence was forty-one when she was released on 25th July 1904. She went out to a world she no longer knew, but to which she seems to have adapted with that remarkable resilience that had helped her to survive the appalling conditions that existed in English prisons at that time.

After spending some time in Paris with her mother, who had nearly beggared herself in trying to obtain her daughter's release, Florence went to America. Her reception on her arrival in New York was more like that of a modern visiting film star, rather than that of a woman who had spent nearly fifteen years of her life in prison. The heady sense of freedom and happiness she must have felt in returning to her own country did not last for long. She wrote a book, *Mrs Maybrick's Own Story: My Fifteen Lost Years*, and she made many lecture tours before life dealt her a couple of devastating blows. Her mother died suddenly in a convent outside Paris, and as if this was not enough, her son died soon after, having drunk from a beaker of potassium cyanide by mistake. To make her life even more financially difficult she then learned that the family properties in Mobile had been taken over by squatters who had held them for so long that it was now virtually impossible to re-establish her claim on them; others had been annexed by the government because taxes had not been paid on them for years. It was about this time she decided to drop out of the public view by reverting to her maiden name of Florence Chandler.

A businessman and a friend suggested that she should spend the rest of her days in a home, and even offered to supply the money to set her up in such an establishment.

'I would prefer to starve in a gutter,' was her characteristic reply.

She eventually obtained a job selling encyclopaedias for the Chicago publishing firm of Schumann and Company, but it didn't last, and she was forced to sell all her personal possessions and eventually became a vagrant before she went to South Kent, Connecticut, to work for Henrietta Banwell, the chicken farmer.

When Florence came to be buried in South Kent on a bleak autumn day in 1941, she at least died among friends, though not all of her own making, being the difficult and cantankerous old lady she had become. The people of South Kent, however, had taken her to their hearts, despite her dismissive attitude towards many who had tried to help her. In fact, she had a number of secret benefactors outside South Kent who had helped her over the years. There was Alden Freeman, a political reformer who had regularly sent her cheques delivered in person by his attorney who arrived at her shack driving a Cadillac, and there was a schoolmistress named Mary Calhoun, who sent her gifts of money, clothing and food for many years without ever learning of Florence Chandler's true identity. She went short of many things during those last years, but true friends were not among them.

The case of Florence Maybrick has been dealt with by many writers, but perhaps no one has written of it in more detail in the popular field than Trevor L. Christie in his book *Etched in Arsenic*, first published in this country by George Harrap & Son in 1961, in which he also deals with the long years of her imprisonment in painful detail. But like so many others, he also leaves the door ajar when discussing the question of her guilt or otherwise, though coming down hesitantly in her favour at the end.

In writing about a crime after so many years have elapsed, a writer can do no more than venture an opinion as to whether she was guilty or not of the murder of James Maybrick. This writer, going against popular opinion, thinks she was probably guilty.

Florence Maybrick was a woman of iron will and extraordinary resilience, which was very far from the impression she gave in those days at Battlecrease House or in the dock. Consider then the position of this strongwilled woman when Brierley came on the scene. She was married to a man whom she no longer loved, and who was a great deal older than herself, but who could still live for more than thirty years, when she would be an old woman with no money of her own, because he had left it all to the children. What woman of any spirit would put up with that sort of situation? She was convinced that Brierley would marry her if Maybrick was no longer around. All she needed was the strength of purpose to do away with him, and that we know she had in full.

Much has been written about the arsenical fly-papers. That she made no secret of soaking them to extract the arsenic has been brought up as partial proof of her innocence. This was not necessarily the action of an innocent woman at all, but of someone who had been brought up in the Deep South, where employers treated their negro servants with scant regard for their intelligence. She soaked the fly-papers in the presence of the servants because she assumed they would not know what she was about. If she had not given that fatally incriminating letter to Miss Yapp to post, she would probably have got away with it, as Maybrick had been filling himself with arsenic for years and supplementing it with all manner of patent medicines which could have led to gastro-enteritis – the original diagnosis of the doctor who had attended James Maybrick, before his brother had called for a postmortem.

There is no doubt that Florence Maybrick was wrongly found guilty on the evidence that was produced at her trial, and that she suffered greatly afterwards. It was also appalling that no Court of Criminal Appeal then existed to overthrow the decision of a jury which had been wilfully misdirected by a judge who was already tottering on the brink of insanity. But in the final analysis, all that is beside the point if she were really guilty of the murder of James Maybrick.

A COSY MENAGE A TROIS

Jean Pierre Vaquier (1924)

When Mrs Alfred Jones arrived in Biarritz, she was in a distinctly unhappy mood. She had put up the money for her husband and herself to become the licensees of the Blue Anchor in Byfleet in Surrey, only to see the business slowly founder, thanks mainly to her husband's mismanagement and his habit of drinking away whatever profits the Blue Anchor might have made. In the November of 1923 their financial situation had become so bad that they now faced bankruptcy, which had led to Mrs Jones having a nervous breakdown. Acting on the advice of her doctor, she informed her husband that she was taking a holiday to get away from it all for a while. 'I hope you can manage by yourself,' she said to him.

'Of course I can,' Mr Jones said absently. 'Take whatever time off you need, my dear.' The couple had been married in 1906, and there had been two children. Marriage had therefore lost much of its original lustre for both of them, and any thoughts he might have had that his wife could have an affair while she was away did not bother him unduly. Apart from anything else, he welcomed the idea of being alone, when he would be free to drink without having to listen to his wife's recriminations whenever he reached for the gin bottle.

As for Mrs Jones, her only thought was to get away from England, after having spent months of futile scrimping and scraping in an attempt to cope with the mountainous pile of bills on her desk. Having decided she would live in some style on this one occasion, she booked in at the Victoria Hotel in Biarritz, an establishment not noted for being eminently suited to the thrifty holidaymaker.

Biarritz was perhaps a rather strange watering place for Mrs Jones to have chosen for her little holiday. Although it has a mild climate throughout most of the year, those who visit it are predominantly the French middle class, who tend to keep very much to themselves and have no great love for the British. Its main attractions for the visitor are the casino, a golf course which has kept going since 1888, and a large sandy beach – none of which was likely to be of great appeal to a married woman past her prime who, moreover, did not speak a word of French. It is difficult to imagine how Mrs Jones would have passed her time in Biarritz if she had not met Jean Pierre Vaquier.

They first met in the dining room of the hotel, where Vaquier was in charge of the radio, and where visitors staying at the hotel could listen to concerts being transmitted from England. Vaquier was attracted to Mrs Jones from the start, but as neither of them could speak the other's language, his attempts to strike up a conversation quickly petered out. After an exchange of inadequate gestures, Mrs Jones regretfully drifted away, only to find Vaquier at her elbow again, when he managed to convey to her that it would be a good idea if she bought herself a dictionary to help them communicate with each other. Mrs Jones was intrigued and flattered by Vaquier's obvious interest in her, and she agreed to see him again, when she would have bought herself a dictionary.

When they met again it was on the sands of Biarritz. What followed was an unlikely and rather strange courtship in which Mrs Jones' newly acquired dictionary was passed to and fro between them while they struggled to maintain some sort of conversation. It was a slow and laborious means of communication, but it seems to have worked. Whatever feelings Vaquier had for Mrs Jones in the beginning, they were as nothing compared to what he began to feel for her now as their companionable walks together brought his ardour up to a point where he felt he had to have her at all costs. Undoubtedly Vaquier had fallen madly in love with Mrs Jones, though on her side she still only regarded him as a good friend.

By the time she returned to England in the following January, their relationship had taken a new turn, thanks to a calculated piece of manipulation on Vaquier's part. At his suggestion she had moved to the more modestly priced Hotel Bayonne. Greatly daring, Vaquier had suggested that he move in with her, and Mrs Jones had weakly agreed, thereby storing up a great deal of trouble for herself in the future. Now that they were lovers in the generally accepted sense of the word, Vaquier's ardour for her did not diminish as is so often the way, but instead he began to assume an almost proprietorial role with her. What had started as a relatively harmless seaside affair was now becoming something of an embarrassment for Mrs Jones.

They had only been at the Hotel Bayonne a week when matters were brought to a head when Mrs Jones received a telegram from her husband, asking her to return immediately. Vaquier pleaded with her to stay, and then seeing that Mrs Jones was determined to rejoin her husband, he announced that he was also going to

England where he hoped to sell the patent for a sausage-making machine he had invented. Seeing that she was stuck with him for the time being at least, Mrs Jones began the journey home with him, stopping at Bordeaux and Paris. While they were staying at the Palais d'Orsay in Paris, Vaquier asked for the address of a good but modest hotel where he might stay in London. She suggested the Hotel Russell, and in an unguarded moment gave him her address in Byfleet before catching the boat train for London, leaving a tearful Vaquier behind.

What sort of man was Jean Pierre Vaquier? Was he a crook on the make, or was he merely an inveterate womanizer? He was neither. He was merely a man who was genuinely in love and who was prepared to stop at nothing – even murder – as long as he gained the woman he loved at the end of the day.

In appearance and manner he was a parody of a typical French stage actor seen in a French farce, where the principal player bounds out of one door and through another in his wild pursuit of a chambermaid trying to preserve her most cherished asset from her demonic pursuer. A short, dapper and extremely vain little man, Vaquier had a genuine claim to being an inventive mechanic. Unfortunately, he was one of those men who is unable to separate reality from fantasy. Unlike the actor in French farce who goes home after the performance to a life of bourgeois respectability, Vaquier played out his whole life as if he were on stage. Looking at the photographs of him today with the benefit of hindsight, Vaquier seems to have been a slightly sinister-looking man who sported a spade beard and a heavy moustache. What Mrs Jones saw in him is something of a mystery.

If Mrs Jones hoped that she had seen the last of Vaquier, she was sadly mistaken. No sooner had she left him than Vaquier set off himself for England. Arriving in London he made straight for the Hotel Russell, from where he sent her the following telegram:

> Arrived from Paris on business. Shall be very pleased to see you at the Hotel Russell and to meet Mr Jones. Perhaps you will inform me what evening.

While this telegram was on its way, Mr Jones had decided that now his wife was back he could afford to take a short holiday himself in Margate. By the time the telegram arrived, Mrs Jones had already been summoned to London to the Bankruptcy Receivers' Office in Russell Square. Its proximity to the Hotel Russell was too much of a temptation for Mrs Jones, who had left the Receivers' Office in a depressed state of mind and felt in need of being cheered up. Unwisely, as it happened, she decided to see Vaquier, with the almost inevitable result that she spent the night with him. It was an action that she was to bitterly regret some weeks later. As for Vaquier, the brief renewal of their affair had made Mrs Jones seem more desirable than ever. Beside himself with passion, he followed her to the Blue Anchor, minus his luggage and his sausage-making machine which the management of the Hotel Russell were holding until he was able to pay his bill. With the aid of the now well-thumbed dictionary, he managed to explain that he had no funds until he sold his sausage-making machine. Beside herself with worry, Mrs Jones advanced him the money to pay the hotel manager, who agreed to send on Vaquier's sausage-making machine and luggage.

Mrs Jones was now in somewhat of a dilemma, with her lover happily ensconced in one of the best bedrooms and her husband now on his way home. Faced with this impossible situation, she did the sensible thing by phoning her husband in Margate and telling him about Vaquier, while carefully omitting any reference to their relationship. Vaquier was already making himself objectionable to the staff, although he had only been there for a few hours. Having spoken to her husband, Mrs Jones then awaited his return home with some apprehension, while fervently praying that by the time he got there Vaquier would be gone. From the way he was walking around the Blue Anchor as if he owned the place, she very much doubted it. In the event, Vaquier was to stay at the Blue Anchor for six weeks before Mrs Jones threw him out.

When Mr Jones did arrive home, he was feeling too ill to be much concerned about Vaquier being there, having caught influenza which had turned to congestion of the lungs through being exposed to one of those bitter winds that sweep along the East Kent coast at that time of the year. Croaking his apologies, he retired to bed immediately, where he stayed for the best part of three weeks, while Vaquier got his feet under the table more firmly than ever.

During the period when Mr Jones was ill in bed, Vaquier did his best to persuade Mrs Jones to leave her husband, only to be put off each time by Mrs Jones, who saw no point in exchanging a near-bankrupt husband for an impecunious Frenchman who had not even attempted to pay for his stay at the Blue Anchor. But although there was part of her that wished to see Vaquier gone, she still wanted him physically, and they remained on intimate terms whenever the opportunity presented itself, generally on the occasions when she accompanied him to London, where he was in the habit of calling in at a chemist in Southampton Row to buy chemicals for his experiments in the field of wireless telegraphy.

When Mr Jones finally rose from his sick bed, he met Vaquier properly for the first time. Unlike his wife, Mr Jones spoke French and the two men seem to have got on well enough until the 28th February, when Vaquier had the audacity to ask him for a loan.

'Don't lend him a penny,' Mrs Jones told her husband. 'He already owes enough on the bill he has run up here.'

On March 1st, Vaquier went to London alone, when he visited the chemist in Southampton Row. As usual, he saw Mr Bland, one of the partners, who also spoke French. He frowned when he looked at the list of chemicals that Vaquier required.

'0.12 of a gramme of strychnine!' he exclaimed. 'That's enough to kill half a dozen men. I can't possibly let you have that.'

'Monsieur, I have bought that item many times in France for my wireless experiments without any trouble,' Vaquier lied. 'It is for the same purpose that I wish to purchase this item again.'

'I suppose it will be all right,' Mr Bland said

doubtfully. 'But you will have to sign the poison book.'

Vaquier signed the book J. Wanker, an odd choice for a false name. But it raised no eyebrows from Mr Bland, who gave Vaquier the strychnine without further comment.

If Mrs Jones had put it more strongly that she had no intention whatsoever of leaving her husband for Vaquier, the events that were to follow might never have happened. As it was, Vaquier was quite convinced that he only had to rid himself of Mr Jones, when he would have both Mrs Jones and the Blue Anchor. The latter was, of course, more of a liability than an asset, though Vaquier was not to know this as Mrs Jones had not discussed her financial affairs with him.

Nothing of note happened until the 28th March, when Mr Jones decided to throw a party. By then Vaquier was behaving more outrageously than ever, interfering whenever Mr and Mrs Jones were having one of their periodical 'spats' and generally making it obvious that he was devoted to Mrs Jones. If her husband suspected that something was going on between his wife and Vaquier, he said nothing.

All the same, it was an uneasy *ménage à trois*, especially for Mrs Jones, who must have been in fear all the time that Vaquier would bring this simmering cauldron to the boil by blurting out that it was his intention to break up the marriage.

By Mr Jones's standards, his party was a great success, with everyone getting roaring drunk. The only solitary spectre at the feast was Vaquier who neither drank nor took part in the general merriment, but spent most of his time glowering at Mr Jones, who was too drunk to notice Vaquier's sullen behaviour. At eleven o'clock Vaquier finally retired to his room, where he was forced to listen to the merrymaking going on downstairs until the party finally broke up around midnight.

On the morning of the 29th, everyone who had attended the party rose late – that is with the exception of Vaquier, who rose at seven and went down to the bar parlour, where he made straight for the bottle of bromo salts that always stood on the mantelpiece for Mr Jones to use when he came down with a hangover. Looking around to make sure no one was about to see him, Vaquier then put some strychnine in the bromo salts before making himself a cup of coffee and settling down in the most comfortable chair in the room, presumably to await Mr Jones's arrival downstairs, when he would be able to watch him drink the bromo salts and collapse in his death throes. The cleaners arrived shortly afterwards and tried to move Vaquier out of the way, telling him that he would find it warmer in the coffee room where the gas fire had been lit. Much to their annoyance, Vaquier gave an expressive shrug and refused to move. After they had tidied the room and left, more people came and went but Vaquier still didn't budge from his chair. Then Mr Jones arrived at last, and, after exchanging greetings with Vaquier, went over to make up his bromo salts. 'Damn it!' Mr Jones exclaimed irritably. 'It won't effervesce.' He stirred the bromo salts a few more times and then downed it in a single gulp. 'My God! They're bitter!' he exclaimed. Mrs Jones came in at that moment and, much to Vaquier's alarm, she tasted it herself, only to spit it out in disgust. She put the bottle away in one of the kitchen drawers and returned to the bar parlour, where she found her husband having a violent fit of vomiting. After calling Dr Carle, their local GP, she helped her husband upstairs to his room, where he lay on the bed, his whole body now racked with convulsions.

When Dr Carle arrived, Mr Jones was still alive, and the doctor did his best to save him during the next half-hour, while Mr Jones continued to convulse. Finally, the twitching body of his patient was stilled at last.

'For God's sake, doctor,' Mrs Jones said in horror. 'What killed him?'

'My guess is strychnine poisoning,' Dr Carle said tersely. 'He was showing all the classic symptoms.' He looked across the body of the dead man. 'There will have to be a postmortem, I'm afraid.'

Unlike so many medical practitioners of his day who seemed to hand out death certificates as freely as they gave prescriptions, Dr Carle had seen Mr Jones die in great agony and was highly suspicious of the circum-stances of his death. When the postmortem confirmed his near certainty that his patient had indeed died of strychnine poisoning, he placed the matter in the hands of the police, who wasted no time in getting to the Blue Anchor. The bottle of bromo salts and the glass were taken away for analysis, when it was found that they had been washed, but not thoroughly enough to remove all traces of strychnine. Although Mr Jones' body had been buried in the Byfleet cemetery for a week by then, the body was exhumed and some of the organs taken away by the pathologist, Bernard Spilsbury, who had been called in by the Home Office. His findings confirmed Dr Carle's original opinion as to the cause of death. Certain now that they were dealing with a case of murder, the police first questioned Mrs Jones, before concentrating on Vaquier, who was taken in for questioning.

At this stage did Vaquier become alarmed by the line of questioning the police were taking? Not in the slightest. Finding himself in the limelight, Vaquier blossomed like a well-watered flower, happily posing for the photographers when he left the police station. Such was his self-confidence that the police began to wonder if they were on the right track. As with so many murderers before him, such as Frederick Seddon (see pages 1-20) it was his overconfidence that led to his undoing. What did distress him was when Mrs Jones told him that he would have to go as the unwelcome publicity was affecting the business.

On 16th April a picture of the self-confident and smiling Vaquier, which he had practically insisted that the press photographers take, appeared in a London newspaper, where it was seen by Mr Bland of the firm of chemists where Vaquier had signed the poison register for the strychnine. Bland immediately went to the police, and on the 19th Vaquier was arrested at the Railway Hotel in Woking, where he had gone when Mrs Jones had told him to leave.

The trial began on Wednesday, 2nd July, and was held at the Surrey Assizes. Vaquier's defence was led by Curtis-Bennett, who had unsuccessfully defended Edith Thompson in the famous Thompson and Bywaters case in 1923, while Edward Marshall Hall was making one of his rare appearances as counsel for the Crown, led by Sir Patrick Hastings, the Attorney General. Presiding over the case was Mr Justice Avory, who was to have little taste for Vaquier's antics in court. The progress of the trial was hampered considerably by the fact that everything had to be translated, and for that purpose the services of H. Ashton Wolfe, the well-known author of true crime stories, had been enlisted. However, the process of translation meant that the points made by the prosecution lost their impact by the time they had reached the jury. Not that this greatly affected their ultimate verdict, for by that time Vaquier's string of obvious lies and his posturing had irritated everyone so much that his fate was already a foregone conclusion.

Vaquier came up from his cell and bounced into the dock, from where he practically took over his own defence. 'The hotel was a house of pleasure,' he informed the court, 'where things happened which are unknown in brothels.' The idea of the highly respectable Blue Anchor being a place where strange acts of perversion were carried out was so ludicrous that his statement was ignored, as were his attempts to implicate the potman, George, in the murder.

'The second act of this drama will be the disappearance of the wife of George, as mysteriously and also as tragically as Mr Jones,' he cried out melodramatically, seemingly oblivious to Avory's pained looks. It says much for British justice that all this nonsense was listened to in silence, rather than being greeted with howls of derision, as it might well have been elsewhere.

Seeing that he was getting nowhere with this line of approach, Vaquier then told the court that he had purchased the poison for Mr Jones's solicitor so that he could destroy his dog, a statement that was so obviously untrue that Avory was to dismiss it outright in his summing up.

The prosecution tried vainly to get the trial back on course. 'I suggest that you were infatuated with Mrs Jones and were prepared to kill for her,' he said.

'That is not true,' Vaquier said hotly. 'I cared for her only as a sister. As for Mr Jones, he was like a brother to me.' No one believed him for one moment.

In the face of all this absurd nonsense, which had also included a statement that Mr Jones had willingly lent Vaquier money until he had sold his invention, Curtis-Bennett could do little for his client, contenting himself mostly with attacking the character of the unhappy Mrs Jones, and calling into question the amount of strychnine that had been found in the organs of the body. None of it made any impression on the jury.

After the jury had listened to Vaquier declaring that the death of Mr Jones had been caused by 'some coward jealous of my presence here', the Attorney General and Curtis-Bennett made their final speeches and then Justice Avory made his summing up, in which he concentrated on the damning evidence of Vaquier's purchase of the poison. In spite of the quality of Vaquier's 'evidence', if such a word can be used for the incredible number of lies he had told the court, Avory was commendably fair to the prisoner throughout the whole of his summing up, when he could have simply demolished the defendant's testimony. The jury then went out to consider their verdict – guilty as charged.

Until that moment, Vaquier had remained supremely confident that he was going to get away with it. On hearing Judge Avory pronounce sentence of death, Vaquier behaved like some actor who has come forward to receive the plaudits of the audience, only to be booed off the stage. His face working with uncontrollable fury, he clung to the dock and launched into a tirade of hysterical abuse until he had to be dragged away, still ranting on about the injustice of his trial.

No sooner had he been delivered to Wandsworth Prison than he was demanding to see the governor; this time he had yet another absurd story in which he stated that he had seen Mrs Jones hide a bottle of strychnine in the toolshed. As a matter of routine the police checked up on his story and did indeed find a bottle of strychnine which he must have hidden away for some future occasion if his first attempt at murder had failed.

When his appeal was heard and dismissed, those who had to listen to it were subjected to a repeat performance by Vaquier, who was dragged away, shouting with impotent fury.

He was hanged in Wandsworth Prison on 12th August 1924, departing from this world shouting '*Vive la France*' as the trap doors opened, a dramatic exit line that must have been rather wasted on the executioner and his assistant, who were too busy keeping clear of the drop to take much notice of Vaquier's final words.

A NICE CUP OF TEA

Graham Young (1972)

When Graham Young went for an interview for a job with John Hadlands, a company specializing in making photographic instruments, and situated in Bovingdon, Herts, no one had bothered to tell them that Graham had just been released from an institution for the criminally insane, where he had spent most of the past nine years after poisoning his stepmother, and attempting to murder his father and sister, and his closest friend, by the same means. Almost as soon as he stepped into the office of the managing director on that morning in 1972, Mr Godfrey Foster was so impressed with him that he immediately offered him the vacant post of office junior.

Mr Foster beamed at the young man who sat in front of him. 'As you're just beginning with us, one of your duties will be to make tea for all the office staff. It'll give you the opportunity to meet everyone.'

'I shall welcome that, sir,' Graham said, unable to believe his luck. His poisoning activities had been seriously curtailed in the institution, and now he was being offered the perfect opportunity to kill off the whole staff of Hadlands – something he had every intention of doing once he was settled in his new job.

'A nice, well-spoken young man,' Mr Foster told one of the members of his staff after Graham had gone. 'He should go far.'

Before going into Graham's poisoning activities at Hadlands, it is worth knowing how he came to be put into an institution, and even more relevant, how he came to be released to wreak murder and panic among the staff of a company that had showed him nothing but kindness.

He started to become obsessed with poisons at the age of twelve, and by the time he was fourteen he was the star science pupil at the John Kelly Secondary School in Willesden, where his science master never ceased to be amazed at Graham's enormous knowledge of poisons, acquired through diligent studying of the dozens of books he had on the subject.

When other boys of his age were becoming interested in girls and were searching for smutty passages to read out aloud to their friends, Graham stayed in his room, planning how to put his dangerous knowledge to good use. To his warped mind, the answer was obvious. He would poison whoever was most readily available, in this case the whole of his family who were shortly to have the benefit of his ministrations.

The first to be sent on her way was his stepmother, who had no sooner expired than Graham was at it again, this time putting belladonna in his sister's tea and sprinkling antimony over his father's food. For good measure a schoolmate was also given the benefit of Graham's expertise. Fortunately, he must have been off form when trying to poison the last three, as they all survived. There is no telling just how many people he might have tried to poison at this stage if his science master had not discovered some poisons in Graham's desk and reported it to the police. A search of his house and an examination of his library made it obvious that they had nipped in the bud the activities of a seriously deranged boy who had been all set to begin a fresh campaign of poisoning in which the survivors of his family would have undoubtedly been murdered later.

At his trial in the July of 1962, Graham openly confessed to the charges against him and in the same year was sentenced to serve fifteen years in an institution for the criminally insane, and even then was not to be released without the Home Secretary's consent. The judge who gave this ruling was Mr Justice Melford Stevenson, and in view of what was to transpire, he was wise in recommending that Graham should be kept locked up for so long.

He was sent to Broadmoor where life seems to have been considerably better for the inmates than it was for those in one of Her Majesty's prisons. Graham had access to most of the daily papers and he could read books supplied to him courtesy of the Berkshire County Library. He was able to watch television in a room set aside for that purpose, and eventually was allowed a radio in his room as well as a budgerigar. It was not the best of ways to sit and watch your life trickle by, but his existence was still one which many 'lifers' would have envied.

Like all the patients in Broadmoor, Graham was assigned to a psychiatrist who reported on a prisoner's progress to the medical superintendent. After serving nine years, Graham was pronounced sane enough to take his place in the world again, and was sent on a rehabilitation course at the Slough training centre, where he was careful to make a good impression on the staff, who also took a liking to him and sent him for an interview at Hadlands with their blessing.

This is not the place to launch an attack on a system of release for the criminally insane, beyond commenting that it does seem strange that psychiatrists who are used to dealing with the cunning psychopath, capable of simulating sanity over a long period of time, are often fooled into believing a patient sane. Graham had been just such a patient, and he was not the first to have been released to carry on his murderous activities.

For his first few months at Hadlands he did nothing beyond carrying out his duties. Much of his work was done with Bob Eagle, who was in charge of the storeroom. Eagle was sixty at the time and looking forward to his well-earned retirement. A hard-working and good-humoured man without pretensions of any sort, he took a liking to Graham and did his best to make him feel at home at Hadlands.

'We're one big happy family here,' Eagle told him. 'Believe me, this is a really nice company to work for. I should know. I've spent most of my life here.' He looked at his watch. 'Time to make tea, Graham.'

Graham dutifully went off to make the tea, but this time he doctored Eagle's tea with thallium, a highly toxic element used as a rodent and insect poison which the Austrian murderess, Martha Marek, had used to dispose of her husband and child and one of her lodgers, and for which she had been beheaded in 1938. Graham had no practical experience of how people died after taking this poison, and it was something he was anxious to try out, together with a number of other poisons in due course.

From Graham's point of view, Eagle's reaction to the

poison was a most satisfactory one. First Eagle began to suffer from violent pains in his stomach and back which were followed by bouts of continual vomiting. Graham continued to dose Eagle's tea with thallium, and his condition inevitably continued to deteriorate, until he was only able to walk with extreme difficulty. His doctor treated him for peripheral neuritis, an understandable diagnosis as this is a disease in which damage is done to the nerve ends in the body, and may be caused by a number of disorders, ranging from alcoholism to certain vitamin deficiencies. Eagle did not respond to treatment, but instead grew steadily worse, until he was finally put in the intensive care unit of St Albans Hospital, where he died in agony.

After attending Bob Eagle's cremation with the rest of the staff of Hadlands, Graham let a couple of months pass before he was at it again, this time putting thallium in the tea of selected members of the staff. As he doled out the poison in varying degrees of strength, it tended to be very much the luck of the draw as to who was to be the unlucky next victim.

This was Fred Biggs, a happily-married man of fifty-six, with four children, and someone who had enjoyed good health until he was struck down by a mysterious illness not dissimilar to the one that was also attacking various members of the staff who were attributing their malaise to the Bovingdon Bug, an equally mysterious bug which had been put down to a form of gastric infection that had laid low a large number of the local schoolchildren for a while. It was the conviction that this bug was responsible for their illness which obscured the fact that they were all being slowly poisoned by someone at Hadlands.

Although he had gone home that night feeling poorly, Biggs returned to the office the next day very much better. He was greeted that morning by the ever-solicitous Graham, with a cup of tea in his hand. 'Glad to see you're better, Mr Biggs,' Graham said. 'Here's your morning cup of tea.'

Before the day was out Mr Biggs was clutching at his stomach and had to be sent home. There is no point in dwelling on Fred Biggs's appalling suffering over the next nineteen days before he died. Considering the circumstances, he had put up a long fight for his life before he finally passed away in the National Hospital for Nervous Diseases in London, the true cause of his death still remaining a baffling mystery to the doctors who attended him.

In Graham's diary, which was found after his arrest, were two significant entries about poor Mr Biggs, who, like Eagle, had died in agony. The first made it obvious that Biggs's prolonged fight for life had worried Graham, who wrote: 'he is surviving too long for my piece (sic) of mind.' If Graham had given more attention to his spelling and less to his books on poisons, none of this might ever have happened.

The second entry in Graham's diary was written when it had become evident that Biggs was going to die. 'It is better that he should die. It will be a merciful release for him, as if he should survive he will be permanently impaired,' Graham wrote. His diary gives an interesting insight into the mind of a young man who killed for none of the classic reasons of revenge, sexual jealousy, or profit, but for no other reason than he wanted to see the effect of a poison on a human body. Never at any time does Graham in his diary show even the slightest remorse or pity for his victims.

The death of Bob Eagle had been depressing enough, but when this was followed by the death of Biggs the staff were thrown into a state of absolute panic, especially as some of them had been taken ill from what they thought was the Bovingdon Bug. They talked of nothing else whenever one of them returned looking wan and shaken after a brief bout of the mysterious illness that was striking at random in their midst. Needless to say, Graham remained untouched by the 'bug' and was beginning to get slightly on everyone's nerves as he portentously talked about their illness, displaying in the process a remarkable knowledge of poisons which would have done credit to a doctor specializing in the subject, let alone a young man of twenty-three. It was only with the benefit of hindsight that they remembered Graham had taken more than a normal interest in Fred Biggs's battle for life in the hospital, going into ghoulish detail of the dying man's symptoms, such as his unbearable agony from the touch of the bedsheets on his legs, facts that he had culled from those who had visited Biggs. At the time, however, they saw it merely as an example of Graham showing off in a way that a callow youth is apt to do when trying to impress older people.

Graham now began to concentrate his attentions on two people: Jethro Batt and David Tilson. This time he upped the doses considerably so that both men were getting between five and eight grains of the poison. The effect of the increased dosages was almost immediate. Tilson began to complain of violent pains in his legs and a feeling of 'pins and needles' in his feet. Equally as alarming was when he began to rapidly lose his hair. Jethro Batt also suffered similar symptoms, and he began to lose his hair. He immediately went into hospital, where he was out of harm's way.

For some reason at this stage Graham became scared of being found out. Why this should have happened is not clear, as both Eagle and Biggs had spent some time in hospital before they had died. In that time they had been under the best of medical attention and the true cause of their illness had still never been discovered. Whatever the reason, he recorded his fear of being caught in his diary, where he wrote: 'I must consider this situation very carefully. If it looks like I'm going to be detected then I shall have to destroy myself.' This was no melodramatic posturing on his part, but was written with deadly earnestness, and he was prepared to back it by taking an overdose of thallium which he carried around with him all the time. What is rather surprising is that if things went wrong for him, he intended to end it all with a poison that would cause him to die in great pain, when other less painful poisons would have done the job just as effectively.

His timing was impeccable, for the management had just decided that the present state of affairs could not go on if they were to keep their staff, some of whom were probably already looking for jobs elsewhere. A team of medical experts was called in to examine every possible source of the bug.

The medical team went through everything, examining air vents and water tanks, and concentrating on the store room which was full of chemicals. They found nothing.

It was then that a member of the team, Dr Arthur Anderson, had a bright idea. He called a meeting of the entire staff and asked them to put forward any ideas they might have as to the cause of the outbreaks of mysterious deaths and illnesses that had broken out at Hadlands. This, too, produced nothing in the way of valuable information. What it *did* do was to turn the spotlight on Graham, who, instead of keeping quiet, began to air his medical knowledge to Dr Anderson. During the countless questions he threw at the doctor, Graham was his old confident self again, and he was even bold enough to ask some pointed questions about thallium. It was almost as if he were trying to guide Dr Anderson in his direction.

Anderson knew little about thallium, but purely as a matter of routine he looked it up in the medical reference books and saw that the symptoms of poisoning by thallium were not inconsistent with those suffered by members of Hadlands' staff. Still following through the possibility that thallium might be the cause of everything that had been going on in the firm, he went back to see Mr Foster and asked if it was used in making any of their photographic instruments.

'Apart from being used as a rodent and insect poison, I believe it is also used in low-melting glass and in the making of photoelectric cells. I thought perhaps you might use it in the making of lenses.'

'Definitely not,' Mr Foster told him emphatically.

'The only suggestion I have to make is that maybe you have a carrier of some sort among the staff,' Dr Anderson said. 'Either that, or you have someone trying to poison the whole of your staff.'

'All my staff have been here for years, and they all get on very well,' Mr Foster told him. 'That is unless someone has a grudge against the management, and somehow I can't see that. We have always made it a policy to treat the staff well. That's why they have all been with us for years. That is, with the exception of Graham Young.'

'What about him?'

'He's too well-liked by everyone for him to want to do anything like that.'

After Dr Anderson had left him, Mr Foster mulled over what he had suggested to him and then went to see his fellow directors. 'The medical team we brought in don't seem to be getting very far with the problem we have here,' he said. 'I suggest we call in the police.'

Once the police had been called in it was only a matter of time before Graham was caught. He must have realized that his days of freedom were numbered, but he still made no attempt to poison himself, even when the police came to his house and searched his room.

'Which one am I supposed to have murdered?' he asked coolly. When questioned about the various entries he had made in his diary relating to his various attempts on the lives of the staff, he contended that they had been notes he had made for a novel he was going to write. It was a feeble excuse and he must have known it, for he eventually admitted to having killed Bob Eagle and Fred Biggs.

'I could have killed the others, but I let them live,' Graham said magnanimously.

Even if Graham had not admitted to the murders, the phial of thallium that was found in his jacket pocket would have been enough for the police to know they had found their man. When taxed with the phial, Graham shrugged. 'That was supposed to be my exit dose.'

His case came to court in St Albans in the June of 1972, when he entered a plea of not guilty, although he had already admitted that he was guilty to the police. Any hope that he might be able to fool the jury, as he had done everyone else so far, was lost when he could not resist airing his knowledge of poisons. The jury listened to him in dismay, unable to comprehend how such a monster could have been released without supervision, or at least letting his employers know that he had suffered with something more than 'a personality problem throughout his adolescence of which he is now fully cured'.

On Graham being found guilty, Sir Arthur Irvine, the defending counsel, put the matter succinctly when he addressed the judge before sentence was pronounced. '. . . That release appears to have been a serious error of judgement, but the authorities now have a duty to protect Young from himself as well as a duty to protect the public,' Sir Arthur said. He then went on to suggest that Graham's condition would be better served if he were sentenced to prison – rather than being sent back to Broadmoor – to which Graham himself had already agreed. Why Graham agreed to this remains something of a mystery unless he thought that one day he might get out of prison, whereas he knew that if he went back to Broadmoor it would truly be until the end of his life. The judge accordingly gave him a life sentence.

Like all psychopaths whose minds run to murder, Graham's crimes were so unfeeling and committed so absolutely without pity that it is impossible to feel anything but relief that he was put away for life.

A CURE FOR IMPATIENT LOVERS

Adelaide Bartlett (1886)

If indeed Adelaide Bartlett did murder her husband, her case must be one of the strangest of all the Victorian murder mysteries, in which the greatest mystery of all was how she managed to do it in the face of what still seems a physical impossibility. After her trial, a distinguished surgeon named Sir James Paget commented dryly, 'Mrs Bartlett was no doubt properly acquitted, but now it is hoped that in the interests of science she will tell us how she did it.' Obviously Sir James thought she was guilty, but his comment opened up areas of speculation on the case which have not been answered to this day. Not only does it seem impossible for her to have administered liquid chloroform to her husband on that fateful day in 1885, but it also seems equally impossible for anyone else to have administered the fatal dose. Come to that, it also seems impossible for Mr Bartlett to have poisoned himself without everyone running to his bedside while he lay dying, screaming in agony.

What helps to make this case so fascinating to the layperson are the additional intriguing ingredients, which include a randy and self-seeking clergyman, a more-than-accommodating husband with a taste for voyeurism, and a very nasty father-in-law intent on ruining Adelaide Bartlett's marriage to his son. With this potentially explosive situation you have a set of circumstances that belong to the darker realms of Victorian domesticity that make the lives of the average modern family seem tame by comparison.

The illegitimate daughter of a French mother and an

English father, who was rumoured to be a member of Queen Victoria's court, Adelaide was born in France in 1855, and spent part of her life there before being dumped on her maternal aunt and uncle, a Mr and Mrs Chamberlain, who were as anxious to get rid of her as her mother had been. Around 1875, Edwin Bartlett visited the house and immediately fell in love with Adelaide. He proposed marriage to her via the Chamberlains who accepted his proposal on Adelaide's behalf, with the proviso that her mother also agreed to the marriage. In those days illegitimacy was a tremendous social stigma, and Adelaide's chances of making a good marriage had been almost non-existent until Edwin Bartlett came along. Her mother was therefore only too happy to see her daughter married in exchange for a lump sum in cash which was paid to Edwin Bartlett in lieu of the usual dowry. During the period these negotiations were going on, Adelaide saw her husband-to-be only once.

Adelaide's parents probably thought they had done well by her, though in truth Edwin Bartlett was no great catch. His new wife was only nineteen and good looking, while he was thirty and only a grocery and provisions merchant in a small way. It did not take his new wife long to learn that he had a number of strange ideas about sex, not the least of them being a desire to keep his wife pure and unsullied. Adelaide therefore returned from her honeymoon still a virgin. His attitude at this stage was not unlike that of the art critic, John Ruskin, when he married an artist's model, Effie, and forced her to endure six years of married life without sex, after he had informed her on their honeymoon that her body 'disgusted' him. Not surprisingly, Effie eventually ran away and married the artist Everett Millais. The way events were to turn out, it would have been better for Adelaide if she, too, had run away from the marriage. It was something that must have also occurred to her as she did try at one time to run off with Mr Bartlett's brother, Frederick, only to think better of it and return to Edwin, who magnanimously forgave her.

Rather surprisingly, to begin with the marriage was not an unhappy one. Whatever faults Mr Bartlett might have had, keeping a woman in a strictly subservient position was not one of them. He was secretly rather proud of the fact that his wife's father was well born, and wanted his wife to be educated and able to hold her own when he moved up in the social strata, which he hoped to do in the not too distant future. He therefore sent her to a school in Stoke Newington for a year, and then afterwards packed her off to a convent school in Belgium for two years.

Towards the end of 1877 she joined her husband in the flat above his shop in Station Road, Herne Hill. No sooner had she arrived than Mr Bartlett senior lost his wife and moved in with them for company. As Adelaide and her father-in-law detested each other, and Bartlett Sr had already made it obvious that he would break up the marriage given the chance, it was an unwise decision on Edwin's part to let him in the flat. Bartlett Snr was a vindictive old man who had never forgiven the couple for not inviting him to the wedding, and he set out to make trouble from the start. His war of attrition against

Adelaide culminated in his accusing her of having an affair with her brother-in-law, Frederick Bartlett. As there had already been some gossip about them, Edwin was anxious to stop his father spreading it any further and sent for his solicitor, and his father was made to sign a letter of apology. Not wishing to be thrown out, the father wisely kept his mouth shut from then on, and for the next five years they all lived in comparative harmony. Considering how much the old man hated Adelaide, it must have taken considerable willpower on his part to be civil to his daughter-in-law. He was to make up for it later.

In 1883 Edwin Bartlett was able to move into a house called 'The Cottage' at Merton Abbey, near Wimbledon, having prospered enough to now own six shops. Much to his annoyance, Mr Bartlett Snr had been told earlier to find other accommodation when the Bartletts had lived for a brief spell in another flat in Lordship Lane, Dulwich. This had been a bitter pill for him to swallow, but he had no option but to accept his son's argument that it was no longer practicable for them all to live together. Mollified to some extent by the fact that his son was always on hand to dole out money should he run out of cash, Mr Bartlett had gone on his way, secretly vowing to have his revenge on Adelaide, whom he blamed for having him thrown out.

In 1885, the Reverend George Dyson became the minister for the local Wesleyan church which the Bartletts used on Sundays. A plump-faced, rather limp young man of twenty-seven with the eyes of a wounded spaniel, Dyson was a graduate of Trinity College,

Dublin, and therefore was presumed to be a man of some education. He also turned out to be something of a cad, a rather quaint word the Victorians were fond of using when referring to someone who was an unprincipled rotter unable to behave as a gentleman should. When he visited the Bartletts in the course of his pastoral duties, Edwin took to him immediately and arranged for him to give his wife regular lessons in Latin, geography and mathematics.

To say that Mr Bartlett was now a wealthy man would be something of an exaggeration, but by the standards of a young clergyman struggling to get by on £100 per annum the sight of the interior of 'The Cottage' stuffed with all the dust-gathering clutter with which the better-off filled their rooms, must have made Dyson feel how lucky he was to have the goodwill of a successful businessman such as Bartlett.

As Mr Bartlett's friendship with Dyson grew, he began pushing Adelaide in the young clergyman's direction, until the day came when he spoke of what was in his mind. 'I want you to become Adelaide's guardian,' he told Dyson in one of those rare moments when the two of them were alone. 'I know you will be a good friend to her when I am dead.'

'Of course,' Dyson murmured, having already decided that he wanted to be much more than a good friend to Bartlett's wife. Although he had only been coming to the house for a matter of a few weeks, he had already fallen in love with her, something that Adelaide encouraged by giving him long, soulful looks over her text books. Dyson knew that if he had read the signals correctly he had been given *carte blanche* to carry on with Mr Bartlett's wife, with her husband's approval and Adelaide's willing acceptance of the situation. It was too much to expect a man like Dyson to do anything else but capitalize on the situation. No sooner had he become aware of what actually seemed to be expected of him than he was crushing Adelaide to his manly bosom at every conceivable opportunity. While all these high jinks were going on, Mr Bartlett was getting himself in a lather in the next room as he visualized what was going on between his wife and Dyson, who had become a lover by proxy. The lovers became reckless, kissing and cuddling each other in Mr Bartlett's presence while he watched them, beaming with pleasure.

When the time came for the Bartletts to go on holiday for a month in Dover, Mr Bartlett was anxious to keep the situation that existed on the boil, and he urged Dyson to visit them as often as he liked, and even offered him his expenses whenever he came. Dyson took advantage of the offer and visited them six or seven times while they were there.

When they returned from holiday, Mr Bartlett went a step further in bringing the lovers even closer together by changing his will. Previously he had left everything to Adelaide on the condition she never married again. If she did, she forfeited everything, a dog-in-the-manger attitude common to many Victorian husbands who tried to rule their wives from the grave. In the new will, Adelaide was free to marry again, with no strings attached. As his successor in the marriage bed, the man Mr Bartlett had in mind was Dyson, and to make sure that Dyson fully understood what was in his mind, he visited him in his lodgings.

'In my new will Adelaide is now free to marry the man of her choice, but it is my dearest wish that you and Adelaide should come together,' he said emotionally.

Instead of being grateful, warning bells began to ring in Dyson's head. It was one thing to have a carefree affair with the wife of a compliant husband, but the last thing he wished for was to find Adelaide on his doorstep, expecting marriage before her husband was even cold in his grave. Realizing that he was getting out of his depth, Dyson tried to back off from a situation which seemed to be now getting out of hand.

'Mr Bartlett, I have to be honest with you,' Dyson said earnestly. 'I have become attached to your wife. So much so that I have reached the stage where I have become too fond of her for my peace of mind. I really think it would be best if we all stopped seeing each other.'

Mr Bartlett brushed all this aside, and Dyson weakly gave in and agreed to continue visiting them.

In the August of 1854, the Bartletts moved to a furnished flat in 85 Claverton Street, Pimlico, where Dyson was made to feel more at home than ever, with his own smoking jacket and slippers kept handy for when he arrived. Dyson still continued to give Adelaide lessons, but whether she learned much was another matter, as the maid who came in every day kept finding them in compromising positions, notably when she found them on the floor together.

All this sexual activity going on in the confines of the

flat began to have its effect at last on Mr Bartlett's hitherto almost non-existent sexual interest in his wife. He now began to insist that she should have sex with him, a demand that Adelaide firmly rejected on account of his nauseatingly bad breath, caused by him having gone to a quack dentist who had sawn off his teeth to the gums and had then fitted him with dentures, with disastrous results. It is perhaps not without significance that she began studying Squire's *Companion to British Pharmacopoeia*, which Mr Bartlett had probably bought on account of his being something of a hypochondriac, forever in search of some medicine with which to dose himself for his mostly imaginary illnesses. It shared the bookshelf with Mr Bartlett's favourite reading – *Esoteric Anthropology*, a book dealing with 'Passionate Attractions and Perversions' among other things.

Two months passed without incident, with Dyson calling regularly at the flat. On 10th December, Mr Bartlett was suddenly taken ill, and Adelaide had to call Dr Alfred Leach, the local practitioner. He found his patient in an extremely depressed state of mind and suffering from diarrhoea and a severe gum infection. Apart from that, Dr Leach found nothing seriously wrong with him, though he did note that the gums suggested that he had recently taken a large amount of mercury. As mercury was the standard treatment for syphilis in those days, Dr Leach asked if he had been treating himself for the complaint, an accusation that Mr Bartlett indignantly denied. At this stage Adelaide seemed genuinely concerned, not so much for her husband, but for herself.

A portrait of the brilliant lawyer, Sir Edward
Marshall-Hall K.C. (1858-1927)

Frederick Seddon on trial accused of murdering
Eliza Mary Barrow (chapter 1)

Eliza Mary Barrow
(chapter 2)

Florence Maybrick,
accused of murdering
her husband James
(chapter 4)

James Maybrick
(chapter 4)

Above: The Byfleet Murder Case – Mrs Jones and children
(chapter 5)

Below: Jean Pierre Vaquier (chapter 5)

Graham Young
(chapter 6)

Below: The
Greenwood Trial
– Sir Edward
Marshall-Hall,
(centre) counsel
for the defence
(chapter 9)

Above: 'Trial By Public Opinion' – Harold Greenwood (chapter 9)

Left: Doctor Hawley Harvey Crippen (chapter 10)

Belle Elmore – Doctor Crippen's wife (chapter 10)

Madeleine Smith
(chapter 12)

Ethel le Neve
dressed as a boy
(chapter 10)

'Everyone will accuse me of poisoning him if he does not get better,' she said worriedly.

It was an extraordinary thing to say, but Dr Leach did not seem to think so as he called in another doctor to examine Mr Bartlett to reassure her that nothing very much was wrong with her husband.

'Get up and get some fresh air, Mr Bartlett,' both of the doctors urged him.

All that Mr Bartlett did was to remain in bed and claim that he felt worms wriggling in his throat. He did, however, get up eventually at the doctor's insistence, saying that he felt much better after seeing a dentist to have some teeth extracted as he had been advised.

The one thing that remained consistent was his morbid state of mind, and when Dyson visited them on the Saturday, he talked in doom-laden tones as if he were about to die. Despite this, Mr Bartlett managed to get through a healthy portion of jugged hare with all the trimmings for his dinner and, for good measure, had a number of oysters for supper.

Dyson visited them the next day, when Mr Bartlett seemed well enough. Dyson stayed with them until the evening and was about to go when Adelaide said, 'I have some letters to post. I'll accompany you to the letter box.'

The two lovers walked through the silent streets together. 'George dearest, would you please be kind enough to get me a bottle of chloroform to sprinkle on Edwin's handkerchief to help him sleep?' Adelaide suddenly asked him.

On the Monday Dyson visited several chemists and

bought four bottles of chloroform which he then transferred into one big bottle, probably for convenience, and then dutifully delivered it to Adelaide. On the evening of the same day Mr Bartlett Sr arrived by invitation to see his son and found him quite well and planning to make an expedition into the countryside in the near future.

New Year's Eve came, when Mr Bartlett ordered a large haddock for breakfast, and generally sounded as if he were on the mend, both physically and mentally. The evening passed quietly enough until bedtime, when Adelaide dozed off in an armchair, while Mr Bartlett went off into a deep sleep.

In the early hours of the morning, Adelaide knocked on the door of her landlord, Mr Doggett. She looked pale and distraught. 'Could you call Dr Leach, please?' she asked him. 'I think Mr Bartlett is dead.'

When Dr Leach and Mr Doggett entered the room they found Mr Bartlett lying peacefully in his bed with a bottle of chlorodyne on the mantelpiece nearby.

'He used it for rubbing on his gums,' Adelaide told them tearfully when asked about the bottle of chlorodyne.

Dr Leach examined the body and was puzzled. 'Is it possible that he poisoned himself?' he asked as he smelt the dead man's lips. He could detect nothing except a very faint smell of brandy which Adelaide explained away easily enough. 'When I awoke I found him lying face downwards. I turned him over and gave him brandy, but I couldn't revive him,' Adelaide told him.

He thought for a few moments, and then said decisively, 'I'm sorry. I cannot issue a death certificate.

There will have to be a postmortem.'

'Of course,' Adelaide said. She seemed as anxious as the doctor was to find out the cause of her husband's death.

By then Mr Bartlett Sr had been summoned, and arrived bristling with suspicion and made a great display of smelling his son's lips to see if he could detect the odour of prussic acid. After kissing his son goodbye, he departed, glaring at Adelaide as he left.

The postmortem was carried out the next day by Dr Green, a well-known pathologist who worked at the Charing Cross Hospital. As soon as he opened the stomach of the dead man, the dissecting room was filled with the smell of chloroform, and feeling the need for further investigation he removed some of the organs for minute examination. On 26th January Dr Leach went to see Adelaide and informed her that her husband had died from swallowing chloroform.

'I wish that anything but chloroform had been found,' Adelaide moaned.

Why ever did Adelaide make that involuntary remark? At this point one can assume the reason. Immediately after her husband's death she had gone away to stay with friends. After being away for four days she returned to the flat in Pimlico where she found the bottle of chloroform that Dyson had bought for her, and had promptly thrown it away. Her reason for doing this depends on whether you think she was guilty or innocent of the crime for which she was soon to be arrested. Either she threw it away because she no longer had any use for it, or because it could provide a vital piece of evidence against her if it were found.

When he heard the results of the postmortem, Dyson agitatedly asked Adelaide what she had done with the bottle of chloroform. 'Oh, damn the chloroform,' she said angrily. She then pleaded with him not to make any mention of the chloroform.

'No!' Dyson said. 'I shall tell the police everything.'

One can hardly blame Dyson for being worried at being implicated in a possible murder case. Even so, he does seem to have behaved rather badly, hysterically even, making it obvious to Adelaide that he now wanted to put an end to their affair. They quarrelled violently, and the row culminated in Dyson asking for the return of the love poems he had written to her. Adelaide responded by tearing them up in front of him and flinging them in his face – an action worthy of a *coup de théâtre* at the Lyceum, noted for putting on melodramas at the time. By doing so, Adelaide was hardly getting rid of some deathless pieces of poetry, if this one which still survives is anything to go by:

> Who is that hath burst the door,
> Unclosed the heart that shut before,
> And set her queen-like on her throne,
> And made its homage all her own,
>   My Birdie.

The end of the affair had come too late for Dyson to save himself. He went away moaning that he was a ruined man, and he was right. At the inquest he confessed to obtaining the chloroform for Mrs Bartlett, and unwittingly gave a

poor picture of himself to the inquest jury, who brought in
a verdict of wilful murder against Mrs Bartlett, with
Dyson indicted as an accessory before the fact. On hearing the verdict, Dyson looked as if he were about to faint.
Adelaide remained composed, as she had done throughout the inquest, showing her contempt for her ex-lover by
studiously ignoring him all the time.

Their trial began at the Old Bailey on 12th April 1866.
Adelaide's father had come forward, and while keeping
his name out of the case, had placed ample funds with
her solicitor to provide her with the best defence lawyer
available. The solicitor had been fortunate enough to
obtain the services of Edward Clarke, QC, MP, whose
spectacular defence of Adelaide Bartlett was to add
immeasurably to his already well-established reputation
as a defence lawyer. George Dyson had Sir Frank
Lockwood appearing for him, while against them both
was Sir Charles Russell, the Attorney General who was
to defend Mrs Maybrick the following year. The judge
was Mr Justice Wills, who was prejudiced against Mrs
Bartlett from the start.

In his opening speech, Sir Charles Russell dropped a
small bombshell by announcing that the Crown now
withdrew their case against Dyson, who scuttled from
the dock with more haste than was seemly, leaving
Adelaide to face Sir Charles alone. Sir Charles then put
to the jury that there were only three alternatives they
had to decide on. Mr Bartlett had either committed
suicide or had taken the liquid chloroform by accident,
or it had been administered by another person. Sir
Charles contended that the first two options were not

possible as Mr Bartlett would have died in such terrible agony that his face would have been contorted. Instead, Mr Bartlett's face was set in repose when he was examined by Dr Leach.

'It is therefore the Crown's contention that Mrs Bartlett chloroformed her husband until he was no longer conscious, and then poured the liquid down his throat,' Sir Charles told the jury. There was only one major flaw in his argument. If Adelaide Bartlett had killed her husband in the manner described, traces of the liquid chloroform would have been found in his wind-pipe which would have been burned as the liquid passed down to his stomach.

The first witness for the prosecution was Mr Bartlett Sr who stepped into the dock intent on seeing his daughter-in-law hanged, and also to dispute the will which was a perfectly legal one, and should not have been brought up in this court anyway. So malevolent was his testimony that it quickly became obvious to everyone that his evidence was worthless. Even the judge, who was not sympathetic to Adelaide, com-mented to the jury that 'very little depends on the evidence of the senior Bartlett'.

As the case proceeded, Sir Charles must have become aware early on that he was fighting a losing battle, though Dyson seems to have done everything he could to make the case against Adelaide even blacker than it was. When it came to questioning him, Clarke handled him with surprising courtesy, whatever his personal feelings about this abject young man might have been. There was a very good reason for this. If he destroyed

Dyson too much in the witness box he would have done his client no good at all, as her own reputation would have been tarnished by association. The only thing that must have worried him slightly was the judge's tight-lipped reaction to all the evidence that was inevitably brought out concerning the peculiar relationships that had existed in the Bartletts' household.

When Dr Leach was called to the witness stand, his evidence was favourable to Adelaide, as he painted a picture of her as a caring and devoted wife whose own health had been beginning to suffer as a result of constantly having to nurse her husband. Mr Bartlett, on the other hand, although a nice man, was always obsessed with the idea of death and had spoken on one occasion as if he wanted to die himself.

'Did you suspect insanity?' Clarke asked him.

'At one time I did,' Dr Leach said. He told them of the occasion he had visited Bartlett when he had related to the doctor how he had got up one evening while Adelaide was asleep in the armchair, and stood with his arms outstretched. 'I stood like this for two hours, and I felt the vital force being drawn from her body into mine, and after that I laid down and slept,' Mr Bartlett had told him.

If not actually insane, Mr Bartlett had undoubtedly been a very weird man in more ways than one.

The most valuable evidence on Adelaide's behalf came, oddly enough, from one of the Crown's witnesses. This was Dr Thomas Stevenson, the Professor of Medical Jurisprudence at Guy's Hospital, who admitted that there was no recorded evidence of anyone committing murder by administering liquid chloroform. If Mrs Bartlett had first chloroformed her husband before pouring the liquid down his throat, it was more than probable that it would have shown in the cerebral ventricles of the brain, Dr Stevenson claimed.

'And you found no such evidence?'

'None,' Dr Stevenson admitted reluctantly.

Edward Clarke pressed on, gradually demolishing the case for the Crown. First, he managed to get Dr Stevenson to admit there was a specific point in time when chloroforming a patient when a doctor knew that his patient was sufficiently anaesthetized not to feel any pain if something like liquid chloroform was poured down his throat.

'How would you know when that time had arrived?' Clarke asked.

'By the reflex action of the eye,' Dr Stevenson said.

'Would you mind showing us how this is done?'

Dr Stevenson obliged by separating his eyelids and touching the conjunctiva.

'That is the test to ascertain if the sensation of pain has gone?'

'Yes.'

Edward Clarke's line of questioning was now becoming clear. Gradually he was establishing that the handling of chloroform in the circumstances put forward by the Crown needed to be done by an expert, and that Adelaide Bartlett did not have that knowledge.

Although he had gone a long way to prove his client innocent, Clarke was still not quite finished with Dr Stevenson. 'Supposing you had to deal with a sleeping man and it was your object to get something down his throat without him knowing it, a liquid that caused great pain, do you not agree that it would be a very difficult and delicate operation?'

'I think it would be an operation which would often fail, and one that might often succeed.'

'But would you not look on it as a delicate operation?' Clarke persisted.

'Yes, I would look on it as delicate.'

By this time Clarke knew that he had the jury on his side, something he exploited to the full when he made his final address to them. Although it was calculated to appeal to the emotions of the jury, it remains one of the most memorable speeches ever made in court, combining, as it did, his remarkable hold on the medical evidence which he used to discredit the Crown, while also making a moving appeal to the hearts of the jury. It was not one of those theatrical barnstorming performances given in the manner of that great advocate Marshall Hall. Clarke's was a more low-key speech, and in its way, more effective.

When it came to the summing up, Mr Justice Wills' review of the evidence was not as impartial as it should have been, and dwelled too much on the unhealthy relationships that had existed between the three principal players. He also dealt at unnecessary length with the book *Esoteric Anthropology*, which he referred to as 'garbage' and 'outpourings of impurity' which must have increased its sales no end. At the end of his summing up it was obvious that he thought Adelaide Bartlett guilty.

The jury thought otherwise, and returned to the courtroom with a somewhat unusual verdict in which they found Adelaide not guilty, while prefacing their verdict with the words, 'Although we think there is the gravest suspicion attaching to the prisoner, we do not think there is sufficient evidence to show how or by whom the chloroform was administered.' In Scotland the verdict would have been 'Not proven'.

A week after the trial, Adelaide wrote to Edward Clarke, thanking him for all he had done for her, and then went back to France for a while before settling in Orléans where she had been born, leaving everyone to wonder if she really had been innocent.

Various people who were involved in the trial gave their views on this intriguing case which still baffles everyone who knows anything about the Bartlett affair.

Edward Clarke was convinced that Mr Bartlett had committed suicide, fearful that he was about to die, while Dr Leach also thought Bartlett had committed suicide out of 'sheer mischief', a statement which does not accord with what we know about Mr Bartlett. Dr Stevenson wrote to Adelaide afterwards to say that he agreed with the verdict.

Most writers dealing with this case today tend to leave the question of her guilt or otherwise in the air. One line of thought that does not seem to have been explored in any detail is the personality of Adelaide Bartlett, who comes across to us through the mists of time as being something of an enigma. We know that she came from a sheltered background and spent two years of her young married life in a convent, which must have given her a narrow view of sexual relationships. Despite this she was able to accept her husband's outlandish views without a word of protest. When Dyson came along and was encouraged by Mr Bartlett to make love to his wife, she took it all in her stride, although she had become used to a sexless relationship, which she may have welcomed, as some women of her time did. No doubt she would have been happy enough for matters to drift along as they were with Dyson and her husband, which would not have affected her economic stability, the uppermost thought in the minds of married women with no money of their own. Certainly, she would never have dreamed of running off with Dyson to live on his paltry income, any more than Dyson wished to be saddled with a wife, as he had made quite clear when his position was threatened.

Then Mr Bartlett had begun to insist on his marital rights, and remained fairly firm on the matter, a fact that is supported by the packet of preventives found in his jacket pocket after his death. The thought of having to live with her literally foul-mouthed husband and share a bed with him was too much for her once it became obvious that Mr Bartlett was not just about to die as he kept claiming he was. At that point she decided to get rid of him and then chloroformed him until he was unconscious and poured the liquid down his throat.

Why then did the liquid not leave burn traces in his throat? For the answer we have to turn to the words of Dr Stevenson at the trial when he said that to pour chloroform down the throat of someone without leaving burn traces would be a delicate operation which would often fail, and would often succeed. Adelaide may well have poured the chloroform down her husband's throat, not knowing that it might leave burn traces, and she was just very lucky it did not.

Many wives have used the excuse of having a headache to deter their husband's sexual advances, but if this theory is anywhere near the truth, Adelaide Bartlett must be the only woman to have used chloroform to deter her husband from making a nuisance of himself.

DEATH AT THE KNICKERBOCKER CLUB

Roland Molineux (USA 1889)

To most people who met him, Roland Molineux must have seemed a charming and debonair young man who had not only been blessed with good looks, but was also lucky enough to have been born into money. His father was General L. Molineux, a highly respected hero of the American Civil War, who had since carved out a career for himself in politics and now lived in an imposing-looking brownstone mansion in Fort Green Place in Brooklyn. His son, on the other hand, was a wealthy nonentity who had made no attempt to study at school, with the result that he did not even reach the academic level required for him to go on to college. As he had his father's money behind him, Roland was not unduly worried, preferring to spend his leisure time in training to become a champion on the horizontal bars, rather than trying to follow his father into politics, which he could well have done with his father's backing. Instead he contented himself with becoming the manager of a paint factory in Newark, New Jersey. Although his job was by no means a glamorous one, Roland made up for it by involving himself in the New York social whirl, where he was welcomed for his good looks and money.

When the Knickerbocker Athletic Club opened in New York in 1895, he was one of the first to join, and there found a friend in Henry Cass Barnet, a broker of thirty-two who sported a distinctive brown beard cut to a point, and was something of an athlete himself, being a yachtsman. Like Molineux, he was a bachelor who could switch on the charm when in female company.

The club had rooms where they could live, and both Molineux and Barnet moved in.

Despite his surface charisma, Molineux was an arrogant and self-opinionated man with a nasty vindictive streak in him. The first person he came up against in the club was Harry Cornish, the main physical athletic instructor in the club. Both men had a high opinion of their sporting prowess, and it was therefore almost inevitable that there should be a clash of personalities. Their mutual hostility eventually flared up into a first-class row, and Molineux stormed off to see the president of the club to whom he complained bitterly, saying that Cornish's high-handed manner was out of place in a paid employee, and demanding that he should be sacked, or else he would resign. Cornish won the day, and Molineux was forced to carry out his threat and left the club. Somehow he managed to get himself elected to the Board of Governors of the New York Athletic Club, leaving Cornish to carry on as before at the Knickerbocker Club.

Two years passed without further incident, with Molineux keeping well out of Cornish's way, though still keeping in regular contact with his friend Barnet. In the spring of 1897 Molineux met the Cheseborough sisters at the New York Yacht Club, where they had been taken by a man named A.J. Morgan, a member of a well-known manufacturing family in New York. One of the sisters was Isia Cheseborough who was married to Walter Sterns, a wealthy Bostonian. The other was Blanche Cheseborough, an attractive and lively 22-year-old girl who was hoping to make a career for herself as

a singer, and had already been auditioned by Jean De
Reszke of the Metropolitan Opera House, and had sung
for Dame Nellie Melba.

Isia was forty, and rather stout, and was not likely to be
of interest to Molineux, even if she had not been married.
Blanche was something else again, and he made for her
like a bee to a flower. The pair of them must have made an
attractive-looking couple as they walked the deck of Morgan's yacht and mingled with the New York rich who
were there to watch the various yachts sail in and out of
Bay Harbour, which had been a favourite rendezvous for
the yachting fraternity for several decades. It was a scene
like something from Scott Fitzgerald's *The Great Gatsby*,
a novel which was to capture the lives of the idle rich in the
'Jazz Age' some thirty years on.

Although Blanche was not short of admirers, she
seemed to favour Molineux, who was not only able to
give her a good time on the town, but was also interested
in the opera, and eventually spoke of sending her to
Paris for singing lessons. Unwisely, he introduced her to
Barnet, who immediately began dating her himself.

To have two well-heeled men about town pursuing
her must have been a heady experience for a girl who
had been brought up in Westerly, a township in Wash-
ington County, better known in those days for its
production of granite than for its sophisticated high life.

On Thanksgiving Day, Molineux proposed to her,
and, much to his surprise, was turned down. Blanche,
however, did continue to see Barnet until June 1898,
when she stopped seeing him and resumed her relationship with Roland, after having been entertained by

General Molineux in his home, where she had suddenly decided that Roland was perhaps the better proposition as a potential bridegroom, after all. The trappings of wealth that surrounded the Molineux family had obviously had a great influence on her decision. Like all young girls in those days, economic security was the governing factor, especially in this case, where the general and his wife were respected and powerful figures who could open doors not available to someone like Barnet.

In the early October of the same year, Barnet received a box of Kutnow's powder at the club, a harmless enough effervescent laxative powder that he sometimes took. The sender's name was not on the package, and thinking it had been sent by a friend, he put it in the drawer to be used at some future date. He did not use it until 1st November, when he took a dose and immediately fell ill. The Knickerbocker house physician, Dr Wendell Phillips, was summoned at once, and he found Barnet propping up the bar and in some considerable pain.

'Those damned Kutnow powders,' Barnet muttered. 'I was a fool to take anything sent by a stranger.' After diagnosing diphtheria, Dr Phillips got Barnet up to his rooms in the club, where he was visited by his private physician, Dr Henry Douglass, who was extremely worried when he saw the condition of his patient, who was vomiting blood. Barnet again made mention of the Kutnow powder, and Dr Douglass sent it away to be analysed, when it was found to contain a large amount of cyanide of mercury.

'Who sent you the powders?' Dr Douglass asked his patient, once he knew the result of the analysis.

'Never mind,' Barnet said weakly. 'I'll attend to him when I get well.'

It did not need a mastermind to guess who had sent the powders to Barnet. His once good friend and rival in love, Roland Molineux, had sent the package as an act of revenge against Barnet for attempting to take Blanche from him. Unfortunately, Barnet did not live long enough to confront Molineux, as he died on the 10th of November.

Less than a month after his death, Molineux and Blanche Cheseborough were married. After the wedding reception that was held in General Molineux's house, the happy couple went off to spend a brief honeymoon at the Waldorf Hotel before going on to live in a boarding house at 257 West End Avenue, from where Molineux commuted daily to the factory at Newark.

Having got rid of Barnet with no awkward questions asked by the police, Molineux then started to make his plans for disposing of Harry Cornish, a man for whom he had acquired a pathological hatred for no other reason than that he had been responsible for Molineux having to resign from the Knickerbocker Club.

On 23rd December 1898, Molineux sent him an anonymous present of a bottle of bromoseltzer laced with cyanide of mercury, tastefully done up in a Tiffany cardboard box which contained a blue bottle resting in a silver bottle holder. When Cornish carefully unwrapped the parcel in the Knickerbocker Club, one of the members saw the label and asked if he could take a dose as his stomach was upset that day. By a rare stroke of good fortune, the club member found the water cooler empty, and was therefore unable to use the bromoseltzer. He returned the bottle unopened to Cornish, who put it aside and then forgot all about it.

He remembered the bottle when he visited the club on 28th December, when he found it on the desk where he had left it. When he departed, he took the bottle and the holder with him and returned to the apartment he shared with his aunt, Mrs Adams, and her daughter, Mrs Rogers. He handed the bottle and its holder to Mrs Adams.

'I don't need this,' he said. 'Perhaps you can find some use for it?'

'Thank you, Harry,' Mrs Adams said. 'I don't know about the bromoseltzer, but the holder will go very well with some of the silver items on my dressing table.'

The next morning, when Cornish was reading the newspaper over breakfast, Mrs Adams came into the kitchen complaining of a headache, and her daughter who was in the room, suggested that she should take some of the bromoseltzer. Cornish mixed some of the powder for her in water and handed the glass to Mrs Adams, who swallowed some and made a face. 'It's very bitter,' she complained.

'I'm sure it's all right,' Cornish said. He took the glass from her and took some himself. He too grimaced. 'It certainly does seem a little strange,' he commented.

After a few minutes Mrs Adams collapsed on the kitchen floor, where she lay writhing in agony. When the doctor was called, she was already dying. While the doctor was attending to Mrs Adams Cornish was overcome by a violent fit of vomiting, bringing up part of the contents of his stomach, which probably saved his life. Although he survived, Mrs Adams died soon afterwards. When the contents of the bottle were analysed and the postmortem had been carried out, it showed that Mrs Adams had died of cyanide poisoning, one of the more deadly poisons not readily available to the man in the street, but not difficult to obtain by someone who was in Molineux's position.

As the police had no reason to suspect Molineux at this stage, he might well have got away with the murder of Barnet and the accidental killing of Mrs Adams, if he had been more careful in covering his tracks. In one respect he was a little unlucky that Cornish had kept the label on the package that had been sent to him, in the hope that he might be able to trace the sender. As it was handwritten it was to be an invaluable aid to the police in helping them to pin the murder on Molineux.

What was of more immediate interest to them was the silver holder and where it was bought. This was not the horrendous task it might have been if Molineux had bothered to buy it out of the county, or had bought a second-hand silver stand. Instead, he bought it on his own doorstep in Newark, where his factory was. Furthermore, it was marked with the maker's name of F. A. Lebkeucher & Co., a local firm of manufacturing jewellers. From them the police were able to obtain the name of the retailers, Hartdegen & Co., who also had their business in Newark, and were able to inform the police that the item had been sold on the 21st December to a red-bearded man. It was fairly obvious that the beard had been a false one.

By this time the press were making the most of the case by giving it banner headlines, asking who had committed this murder without motive. The New York *Journal* went a stage further by offering $5,000 reward for information that might lead to the arrest of the murderer.

Meanwhile, George W. McClusky, the chief of detectives of the New York police, had already got near to solving the case after he had interviewed Harry Cornish at the Knickerbocker Club. When asked if he had any enemies, Cornish remembered his quarrel with Molineux. Though their quarrel seemed an unlikely motive for anyone attempting to murder him he told McClusky about it. This provided a possible motive, but what McClusky needed was proof if he was to have a case against Molineux.

Then the New York *Journal* flushed out two unexpected witnesses – Joseph Knoch and Nicholas Heckmann, both of whom came forward and told the police they operated accommodation addresses which were used for a variety of reasons by their clients, including the delivery of advertisements offering aids for such sexual debilities as impotence. Knoch told the police that he had rented a mailbox to a man named Cornish, while Heckmann had rented one to someone named Barnet, whose murder was now common knowledge. The firms dealing with such items were all approached, and a firm in Cincinnati was found who said they had received an order for a bottle of potency pills from

H.C. Barnet on the 31st May, and another similar order from H. Cornish on 21st December, the same year. The signatures were in the same handwriting and were the same as the writing on the package that had been sent to Cornish.

The matter was placed in the hands of the District Attorney, Asa Bird Gardner, an old friend of General Molineux. The general was involved at the time in trying to expose the wholesale corruption that was going on in City Hall, and as Gardner was involved the situation was therefore a delicate one as he had no wish to antagonize the general by accusing his son of murder. The best he could do at this stage was to put the onus on the findings of the coroner at the inquest of Mrs Adams, and have Molineux subpoenaed to testify before the coroner's jury.

Once he became aware that Roland was now the chief suspect, General Molineux began to arrange for the family to close ranks. Roland and Blanche were brought into the house to live, and the family began to behave as if they were under siege, which in a sense they soon were, with the press camped out on their doorstep during most of the months that followed.

As far as the Molineux family was concerned, the results of the coroner's inquest were a disaster, with Molineux being arrested for the crimes by order of the coroner, and taken to the Tombs, where he was formally charged with the murders of Mrs Adams and Barnet.

The trial of Roland Molineux began on 14th November 1899. For his defence, General Molineux had acquired the services of George Battle & Bartow Weeks, a very exclusive firm of lawyers who were lured into taking the case by General Molineux saying that he would spare no expense in the defence of his son. Against them was the Assistant District Attorney, James Osborne, who was to make his reputation with this case. Presiding over the trial was Recorder Goff.

Although more than a hundred witnesses were called, and the prosecution's final address alone lasted for more than two days, the case was really an open and shut one from the beginning, and one in which Osborne concentrated largely on establishing that it had been Molineux's handwriting on the package that he had sent to Cornish. All that the defence could do was to move that the case be dismissed for failure of proof.

In his final speech to the jury, Osborne went over the facts, gradually tying together the threads of the case for the prosecution, in which the evidence pointed conclusively to Roland Molineux being responsible for the deaths of Mrs Adams and Henry Barnet. It was a masterly performance marred only at one point by Osborne putting too much emphasis on Molineux's impotence, which, strictly speaking, had no relevance to the case. 'Think of the nights of debauchery – think of the nights of sexual depravity, that must have brought a young man to such a pass that he needed a remedy for impotence,' he said dramatically. The idea behind this line of thinking was to make out that Molineux was a degenerate, and in that he succeeded, going by the looks of disapproval that the jurors cast in Molineux's direction.

After asking for a verdict of guilty, Osborne finally sat

down and the jury went out to consider their verdict. After being out for eight hours they returned with a verdict of murder in the first degree. Three weeks later sentence of death was passed by Recorder Goff, and Molineux was taken to Sing Sing prison to wait for the sentence to be carried out.

Once she knew the verdict, Blanche wanted to leave the Molineux house and get on with her life, but General Molineux pleaded with her to stay, and she reluctantly agreed to remain.

Molineux's defence lawyers immediately lodged an appeal, and more than a year and a half passed before a judgment on the case was delivered, on 15th October 1901. Amazingly, in view of the evidence against Molineux, the verdict was set aside and a new trial was ordered.

The new trial began a year later on 13th October 1902. James Osborne appeared once more for the prosecution, while Justice Lambert presided over the proceedings. This time the defence produced a vital witness who claimed that Molineux was with him at Columbia University on the day that the package had been sent to Cornish. Molineux took the stand for the first time and remained unflustered throughout a five-hour examination. He was defended this time by Frank S. Black, a former governor of New York State, who made a far better defence on Molineux's behalf than his former defence lawyers, even coming up with the suggestion that Cornish was the murderer, and that he had murdered Mrs Adams so that he could marry the daughter. This preposterous nonsense was ignored by the jury, who found Molineux not guilty.

When Molineux walked out of the court a free man, he stepped out into a city that was changing rapidly. Many of the old buildings were gone, and parts of the city were in decay and in danger of becoming genteel slums, including the area where General Molineux lived. Even the Knickerbocker Club was in financial trouble and was shortly to be pulled down and replaced by the Empire State Building. More to the point, as far as Molineux was concerned, Blanche was gone, having broken free at last from the Molineux family, and had taken herself off to Sioux Falls in South Dakota, from where she obtained a divorce from Roland Molineux.

Considerably miffed at Blanche's behaviour, the Molineux family had no more to do with her. Up to her departure, General Molineux had given her a generous allowance, but this stopped from the day she left New York, and she never received another cent from the family.

Soon afterwards she married Wallace Scott, who had represented her in her divorce suit. According to Jane Pejsa, who was fortunate enough to be given access to Blanche's account of her experiences, and used them as a basis for a book entitled *The Molineux Affair*, first published in this country by Judy Piatkus Ltd. in 1983, Blanche's life from that point onwards was a series of disasters. After her marriage she tried to pursue a musical career in New York, only to be balked by the Molineux family who threatened to sue if she appeared under the name of Blanche Molineux, a name which would have given her a considerable pulling power at the box office. She returned to Sioux Falls, and later moved with her husband to Minneapolis. Here their young son died of rheumatic fever, and a year later she and Wallace were divorced.

After the divorce she went at long last to study singing in Paris, where Molineux had once promised to send her. At the age of fifty she returned to New York, where she found she was just not good enough to sing professionally in the highly competitive musical world of that city.

In 1926 she returned to Minneapolis, where she was reconciled to Wallace Scott, only to lose him in an automobile accident in 1930. To make matters worse for her, Wallace left no assets, and she learned that even the house belonged to her husband's relatives under a trust that terminated with his death.

She spent the rest of her life in Minneapolis, living in a series of apartments and trying to keep her head above water, while her meagre reserves dwindled away to practically nothing. Like Mrs Florence Maybrick, she became an elderly eccentric until her death at the age of eighty in 1954.

And what of Roland Molineux, who had indirectly been the cause of so much unhappiness in her life? While he had been in prison he had three books published, including *Death Chamber Stories*. In the outside world he tried with some success to pursue a literary career, bringing out a historical novel, before turning to write a play, *The Man Inside*, which was staged by David Belasco and had a run at the Criterion Theatre in 1913.

Soon afterwards he had what is euphemistically called a nervous breakdown, and General Molineux had the unenviable task of committing his son to King's Park Hospital for the Insane. Roland Molineux died there on 2nd November 1917, due to 'a syphilitic infection, followed by progressive mental deterioration, leading to complete dementia'.

After she had left Molineux, Blanche's life may well have been an unhappy one. But as events turned out, it could have been even worse than it was.

TRIAL BY PUBLIC OPINION

Harold Greenwood (1920)

The main interest in this case lies not so much in whether or not murder was committed, as in the cases of Adelaide Bartlett and Mrs Florence Maybrick, but far more in the courtroom performance of that great advocate, Marshall Hall, who managed to save his client after he had been tried and found guilty by local opinion before the trial had even begun. The accused may well have been guilty as charged, but this is of minor importance to the other story in this case of how prejudice brought the prisoner to within a few steps of the gallows far more effectively than the efforts of the police.

The accused was Harold Greenwood, a solicitor from Yorkshire who had come to live in Kidwelly, a now thriving town some thirteen miles from Carmarthen in South Wales. After moving into the town in 1898 he bought himself a modest legal practice in the nearby town of Llanelli. He soon found himself not liked by the Welsh, though his wife, Mabel Greenwood, got on well enough with them. When the Greenwoods had arrived the hostility towards them was very much beneath the surface, and was based mostly on a dislike of outsiders – an attitude that can still be found in certain parts of North Wales.

Despite having to live and work in an atmosphere of suspicion and hostility, Greenwood managed to earn a modest income which he was able to supplement with the annual interest on some money his wife had inherited. It was not a fortune to live on, but it was enough to enable them to buy Rumsey House in

Llanelli, where they brought up four children.

By 1919, Greenwood was still there, and without a single friend outside his local pub in Kidwelly, where people were quite prepared to chat with him over a drink, but never allowed it to go any further.

In Llanelli, however, he did have the Jones family, with whom he was on genuine good terms. The family owned the local newspaper, the *Llanelli Mercury*, which was very close to his own office, and he seems to have had a more or less permanent invitation to lunch with them.

It would be unfair to place the general feeling of dislike that Greenwood's presence generated at the doorstep of the fiercely nationalistic attitude of the Welsh people. The truth of the matter was that Greenwood was something of a womanizer, which did nothing to endear him to the local people, who were mostly devout chapelgoers. Seemingly unaware of the mounting ill will against him, Greenwood carried on as he had always done, adding to the bill that was to be presented to him at the time of his trial.

If Mrs Greenwood knew anything about it, she said nothing, no doubt because she was in ill health and was also convinced that she was suffering from cancer. There is nothing like being certain that you are shortly to die to concentrate the mind on matters far more important than an erring husband. Until then she had been an active member of St Mary's Church, which must have done her a power of good with her neighbours and had probably been responsible for her being accepted in the community.

When she first became ill she was the patient of Dr Griffiths, a hard-working medical practitioner whose medical knowledge fell somewhat short of what was needed to diagnose the cause of death in a patient who had been poisoned with arsenic. When she told him she was suffering from severe internal pains and that she suspected cancer, he did not suggest an X-ray but told her instead that now she was forty-seven she was probably suffering from the effects of the menopause, or that she had a small internal growth.

Clearly Greenwood was not satisfied with this as he suggested that his wife should write to her brother and get him to come down from London with a specialist. His wife agreed to do so, but as with so many people who are unable to face an adverse report on their condition, the letter never got written, and it was left to Dr Griffiths to treat her with palliatives. It says much for Greenwood's indifference to his wife's health that he did not bother to write to the brother himself. After her death he commented that he had felt himself that she had not long to live. Were these the words of a murderer trying to throw up a smoke screen to conceal his crime, one wonders, or merely the remarks of a callous man who had just stood by while his wife slowly died before his eyes?

Sunday, 15th June 1919 promised to be a typical Sabbath day for the Greenwood family. Once breakfast was over, his daughter Irene pottered around the house for a while and then went out into the garden where she read a book. As Mrs Greenwood was feeling too ill to attend church and the car was not being used, Greenwood spent

part of the morning cleaning and overhauling his car.
Lunch was the usual Sunday joint. The Greenwoods were
fond of having wine with their meals, and Mrs Greenwood had a glass of burgundy. After the maid had cleared
the table, Mrs Greenwood went upstairs to have a nap
while Greenwood spent part of the afternoon dozing over
a book in the garden. So far it had been one of those typical
stultifying days that once made Sundays a dog day for so
many people who were not churchgoers. Boring though
they might have been, they were the last hours that Mrs
Greenwood would spend peacefully with her family before her long night of agony that went on until her death
early the next morning.

The sequence of events which followed is revealing in a
number of ways, and seems to reflect again on Greenwood's cavalier attitude towards his wife's illness, and
also to some degree on Dr Griffiths' capability as a doctor.
It was unfortunate for him that after a lifetime of devoted
service to the community he should have been involved in
this case just after he had officially retired, and was only
still attending Mrs Greenwood because she was a patient
of some sixteen years' standing.

In the late afternoon the maid served afternoon tea, and
Mrs Greenwood still seemed in a reasonable state of
health, though she had complained of having had diarrhoea some time after lunch, which she had attributed to
some gooseberry tart she had eaten. Whatever it was that
had given her the stomach upset, it was hardly likely to
have been the gooseberry tart, as it would have taken a
longer period than that to have had an effect on the
bowel.

Before the maid left she saw Irene and Greenwood taking a final stroll around the garden at about six thirty. It was then that Mrs Greenwood complained of feeling unwell again, and her husband gave her a little brandy, which only caused her to vomit. Dr Griffiths was called in and immediately suggested that she should be put to bed. Instead of staying at his wife's bedside, Greenwood went downstairs and played clock golf in the garden with the doctor. Before he left, Dr Griffiths went up and examined his patient, and then went back to his house, which was almost opposite the Greenwoods'. A little later he sent over a bismuth mixture, under the misguided impression that his patient's illness was nothing more than a gastric attack. Mrs Greenwood was suffering from something far more serious.

Soon after the doctor had gone home the Greenwoods had an unexpected visitor. This was Miss Phillips, the local gossip, known to her friends and others as the 'Kidwelly Postman'. If she had been expecting to pick up something to spread round the town, she could not have arrived at a better time. No sooner had she rung the bell than Greenwood arrived at the door.

'My wife is very ill,' he announced. 'Run upstairs and see if there is anything you can do, would you?'

When Miss Phillips came down from the bedroom with Irene, who had been at her mother's bedside, Irene suggested they call in Nurse Jones, who had attended Mrs Greenwood before, when she had been taken ill with one of her heart attacks. Thrilled at being in on this life-or-death drama, Miss Phillips went off to fetch the nurse, who returned with her to find Mrs Greenwood in a state of

near collapse. Nurse Jones told the family that Dr Griffiths should be called at once.

Greenwood does not seem to have shared in the general
alarm at his wife's condition, as he spent so long chatting
with the doctor's wife that Irene had to go over to see what
was happening.

At eleven in the evening, Miss Phillips reluctantly went
home, thereby missing the best part of the story she was to
relate in some detail to her neighbours. Greenwood accompanied her to the gate, where she met Dr Griffiths who
was returning from a late-night stroll before retiring to
bed.

'How is your wife now?' Dr Griffiths enquired.

'Getting better, I think,' Greenwood said casually.

Meanwhile, in the house events were moving inexor-
ably to their end. Around one in the morning, after a nightmare session of non-stop diarrhoea, Mrs Greenwood was
bravely facing up to the possibility that she might die.

'I wish I could have lived to bring up my children,' she
said weakly to Nurse Jones, who was still at her bedside.
'If I don't recover, I would like my sister to bring them
up.'

Apart from Irene, Nurse Jones is the only one who
seems to have come out well in the affair. While she sat
through the night, trying to comfort Mrs Greenwood, Mr
Greenwood was still behaving as if nothing very serious
was going on in the upstairs bedroom. Even Dr Griffiths
does not seem to have been unduly disturbed by his patient's condition when he came over again to see her soon
after she had spoken to the nurse of the future of her children. Instead, he gave her a couple of pills to make her

sleep, and then went back to bed.

Mrs Greenwood died at 3.30 a.m. and Dr Griffiths was called in the next morning, and after examining the body issued a death certificate in which the cause of death was given as valvular disease of the heart. According to Nurse Jones, Greenwood did not seem unduly upset by his wife's death.

It was Nurse Jones who first voiced her suspicion that there was something not quite right about Mrs Greenwood's death, and even more remarkable was Mr Greenwood's seeming indifference to his wife's last illness. She first spoke of it to the Reverend Ambrose, who confessed that he had some doubts of his own over Mrs Greenwood's sudden death. Who carried the story further can only be a matter of conjecture, though it was probably Miss Phillips, who had a nose for a story which most journalists would envy. Whoever it was, the story became the subject of whispered conversations over the tea cups.

After Mabel Greenwood had been buried on 19th June, her husband arranged for her sister, Miss Bowater, to come down from London to look after them all at Rumsey House. The situation soon proved to be an unsatisfactory one, as Miss Bowater began to get on Greenwood's nerves. He was convinced, moreover, that she was turning the children against him, and he decided to send her packing. Once she was gone, his thoughts turned to marriage again, and within four months of his wife's death, he married Miss Gladys Jones, the daughter of the proprietor of the *Llanelli Mercury*, where he had been in the habit of lunching with the family when Gladys was little more than a child.

If tongues had wagged quietly in the privacy of their homes, they now began to clack openly, making wild allegations about his behaviour which bore no relation to the truth. This time there was no attempt on the part of the gossipmongers to keep their tittle-tattle among themselves. Now they talked across shop counters and in the market-place, saying quite openly that they were sure Greenwood had murdered his wife.

The last people who seemed to have heard any of these rumours were the police, who eventually called on Greenwood on 24th October. On a second visit Police Superintendent Jones informed him they would probably ask for an order to exhume the body and arrange for a post-mortem to be carried out.

'Just the very thing,' Greenwood said heartily. 'I am quite agreeable.' The organs were sent to the Home Office for examination by Dr Webster, who in turn passed them on to Dr Willcox, who had already appeared as a key witness for the prosecution in a number of famous murder trials. Both men found that the organs contained a little more than a quarter of a grain of arsenic.

Once the case became public, the press arrived in force to see if they could get a story from Greenwood, who put the situation in a nutshell to a journalist from the *Daily Mail*.

'I am the victim of village gossip, of village scandal, and if you know village life in Wales, you'll know what that means,' he said indignantly.

The *Llanelli and County Guardian* also sent someone to see if there was any truth in the story going around that he had insured his wife's life for £10,000.

'She was not insured for a brass farthing,' Greenwood snapped as he showed the journalist the door.

Events, by and large, do not move very fast in Wales, and it was not until almost a year after Mrs Greenwood's death that the inquest was held. The air inside and outside the Kidwelly Town Hall was electric. Such was the open hostility of everyone who had gathered there that the coroner felt obliged to comment, 'You are not undertaking the trial of Mr Greenwood. You are not a jury in a criminal court where these matters are dealt with according to the strict rules of evidence.'

If the remark was meant to place matters in their proper perspective and dampen down the atmosphere of hostility towards Greenwood, which was as palpable as a solid wall, it had the reverse effect. In fact, feelings were running so high against Greenwood that the police felt it necessary to go to Rumsey House to protect him from any possible violence.

The jury returned with the verdict that everyone had suspected, and indeed hoped for – the death of Mabel Greenwood was caused by arsenical poisoning administered by Greenwood. The verdict was greeted with loud cheers and clapping from the public inside the hall. As he was duty-bound, the coroner ordered a warrant to be issued for the arrest of Harold Greenwood.

As soon as it became known that Greenwood was to be arrested, a large crowd ran whooping through the streets and awaited his arrival at the police station. As soon as he appeared, he was greeted by a barrage of boos and hisses that continued long after he had been taken inside.

Something of this hatred for Greenwood emerges in an

exchange between Greenwood's solicitor, Mr Ludford, and Miss Phillips, at the full-scale inquiry that was held at the Llanelli Town Hall.

'When was the last time that you saw or heard any differences between Mr Greenwood and his wife?' Mr Ludford asked.

'I cannot remember,' Miss Phillips said between pursed lips.

'Try and remember when you saw any differences between them,' Mr Ludford said patiently.

'I'm not going to answer that question,' Miss Phillips said.

Mr Ludford looked taken aback. 'What did you say?' he asked incredulously. 'You refuse to answer the question?'

'Yes.'

'Is that your attitude?'

'It looks like it,' Miss Phillips said indifferently.

'An unpleasant one, isn't it?' Mr Ludford felt moved to comment. He continued to press Miss Phillips on the subject, and finally gave up in despair when Miss Phillips said amazingly, 'It has nothing to do with you.'

One has the feeling that if lynch law had prevailed in those days, Greenwood would have ended up swinging at the end of a rope from a lamppost. Instead, the crowd outside the Town Hall contented itself with sending him back to his prison cell to the accompaniment of more jeers and catcalls after the magistrate had ordered the accused to be committed for trial at the next Carmarthen Assizes.

In all this, Greenwood was lucky at least in having Mr

Ludford as his solicitor. He had not only represented him ably at the hearing, but he also managed to obtain the services of Marshall Hall for Greenwood's defence.

Greenwood was brought to trial on 1 July 1920, and Marshall Hall checked in the night before at the Ivy Bush Hotel, where everyone of importance connected with the case was staying, to say nothing of the press, including some reporters from America who had been sent over to cover the trial. The next morning Hall went to see the prisoner and came away with the distinct feeling that he could well create an unfavourable impression if he were put in the witness stand.

When he arose on the morning of the trial, Marshall Hall was a sick man, and was in great pain most of the time. This did not prevent him from fighting for Greenwood's life with his customary devotion to his client's interests. Against him was Sir Edward Marlay Samson, while Mr Justice Shearman presided over the court.

Hall knew that he had a formidable task ahead of him in trying to prove his client was innocent. The weight of public opinion was against Greenwood and this was bound to have some effect on jurors who could not be depended on to review the evidence in a completely unbiased manner.

A great deal of the first day of the trial was spent in the prosecution filling in the background of the case, while Marshall Hall contented himself mostly with questioning the parlour maid, whose memory after a period of a year was understandably a little hazy, and proved to be of little use to him.

It was not until Miss Phillips took the stand that Hall rose to do serious battle with a witness. Again, he concentrated on the bottle of burgundy, as he had done with the parlour maid.

'Was there any wine on the table the night you were there?' he asked.

Miss Phillips shook her head. 'I know there was no wine on the table that night. If there had been I would have had some.'

If she had been expecting to raise a laugh with that comment she was to be disappointed. The attention of the jury and the public inside the court had already begun to be gripped by the story that was being unfolded before them, and they had little time for light relief – least of all from Miss Phillips, whose previous evidence showed that she was hostile towards Greenwood.

But it was for Dr Griffiths that Marshall Hall reserved the main brunt of his attack. When the doctor stated that he had given Mrs Greenwood two opium pills to make her sleep, Marshall Hall swung round to the court, a triumphant glint in his eyes. 'The evidence that the witness has just given is entirely different to that he previously gave to the police when he said he gave his patient morphia pills.'

'When I said morphia pills, I meant opium pills,' Dr Griffiths said.

'If you had given her two and a half grains of morphia, you would not be surprised if she had died?'

'Yes, I would.'

At this point the court adjourned until the next morning, when Marshall Hall took up his examination of Dr Griffiths at the point where he had left off.

'Now, Doctor,' Hall said. 'There is an enormous difference between opium and morphia.'

'I know that.'

'You said yesterday, when I asked you if it would have been safe to give Mrs Greenwood two and a half grains of morphia, that it would be perfectly safe.' He added helpfully, 'Did you think I meant opium then?'

'Yes.'

Having got Dr Griffiths to admit that he had made a mistake in his original statement to the police, Marshall Hall then proceeded to make life even more difficult for him by implying unfairly that he had given Mrs Greenwood the wrong pills.

'Have you the smallest doubt that if you, as a medical man, had given the patient two and a half grains of morphia after ten o'clock, she would have been dead before four o'clock?'

'If I had given her morphia, she would, but I did not give her morphia,' Dr Griffiths asserted.

Later, Hall asked for a copy of the prescription for the bismuth, only to be told that Dr Griffiths no longer had it. It was not an important point, but it served to throw further doubt on the reliability of Dr Griffiths as a witness.

The next day Marshall Hall pulled one of those little masterstrokes for which he was already famous. Before coming to court the next morning he went to a chemist and obtained a small bottle of Fowler's solution of arsenic, and another bottle of bismuth. When the time came for him to cross-examine the pathologist, Dr Willcox, Marshall Hall asked him innocently what

Fowler's solution of arsenic looked like.

'It's a reddish solution,' the pathologist told him.

'Rather like this?' Marshall Hall asked, producing the bottle of Fowler's solution of arsenic.

'Yes,' Willcox agreed.

'If by some unfortunate mistake the doctor gave Mrs Greenwood four tablespoons of Fowler's solution, you would have got the arsenic you found in her?'

'Yes.'

'And there would be no distinction in the colour of the mixture whether the mixture was of bismuth or of Fowler's solution?' Marshall Hall enquired.

'No, they resemble each other.'

'Like these do,' said Marshall Hall triumphantly, producing the bottle of bismuth and placing it beside the bottle of Fowler's solution of arsenic. He knew that although Dr Griffiths kept both the bismuth and the Fowler's solution in his dispensary, it was extremely unlikely that he would have made a mistake of this nature. But he was fighting for his client's life and the means justified the end, in that he had scored an important point in Greenwood's favour.

His final blow for the defence came at the very end of the trial, when he had Irene Greenwood called to the witness stand.

'Who sat down to supper that night?' she was asked.

'Miss Phillips, Daddy and I,' Irene said.

'What did you drink for supper yourself?'

'I drank burgundy.'

'Was that from the same bottle that was on the table for lunch?'

'Yes.'

The implications from these remarks were obvious. In the first place they proved that Miss Phillips was lying, or had forgotten, when she had stated there was no bottle of wine on the table. Far more important, they proved that if Irene had drunk from the same bottle from which her mother had taken a glass of burgundy, it could not have contained arsenic. With those few simple statements, Irene had saved her father's life.

It was at this point that the judge made a comment, drawing attention to something that was beginning to become obvious to almost everyone in court.

'Is it possible that arsenic was administered, but did not cause death?' the judge asked.

'My contention is that the prisoner never administered arsenic at all,' Hall told the judge.

The judge shrugged. 'If he did not, then there is an end to the case.'

One of the amazing things about this trial, which had turned out to be something of a cliffhanger for those listening to the evidence, is that the prosecution had never once bothered to call Irene Greenwood to the stand, but had relied instead on the evidence of the police who had not bothered to ask those vital questions concerning the bottle of burgundy. Even Marshall Hall did not interview her in private until the closing stages of the trial. When she told him what she was to repeat in the courtroom, he realized that her evidence threw out nearly everything that had been said by both the prosecution and defence counsels. Sometimes in a trial of this nature, where so much emphasis is laid on the medical evidence, the most obvious questions do not always get asked.

In his final speech for the prosecution, Marlay Samson desperately tried to cobble something together from the shreds of the case by pointing out that Mrs Greenwood had also drunk tea and brandy that day, but he knew he was now fighting a losing battle.

Marshall Hall's last speech for the defence went on for more than three hours. As usual, it was in part a serious analysis of the case for the prosecution, which he said had now been blown away in the face of the evidence, and part theatrical performance which the public had come to expect from him. He ended by quoting from the famous speech from Shakespeare's *Othello*, beginning with the line, 'Put out the light, and then put out the light.'

'Are you going, by your verdict, to put out that light?' he demanded in ringing tones. 'Gentlemen of the jury, I demand at your hands the life and liberty of Harold Greenwood.'

After Justice Shearman's summing up on the following day, Marshall Hall felt too ill to wait for the verdict, and went off by private car to Cardiff, where he caught the train to London. At Liverpool Street station a porter came up to him: 'I see you have got him off, Sir Edward.'

Despite Marshall Hall's magnificent defence of Harold Greenwood, there were still many people who thought he was guilty and was very lucky to have got away with it. Of all the people who had been defended by Marshall Hall there was not a single person who did not write to him afterwards to thank him for what he had done for them – that is with the one exception of Harold Greenwood, who never wrote a word of thanks to him for saving his life.

Unfortunately, after the blaze of unwelcome publicity that the trial had brought him, Greenwood's practice rapidly dwindled, and he was forced to move. He went to live on the outskirts of Ross-on-Wye in Hereford, where he assumed the name of Pilkington. He died there a broken man in 1929, at the age of fifty-five.

No one can really be sure that he did not murder his wife, though there seems to have been no motive for him to have done so. Unless, of course, he had merely got tired of her. Greenwood was a very unpleasant man from all accounts, despite his hearty exterior.

Marshall Hall went on to appear in a number of famous murder cases, including successfully defending Madame Fahmy at her trial which is dealt with in the author's book *Fatal Passions*. Marshall Hall was to remember the trial of Harold Greenwood for the unexpected little bonus it had brought him. Before going down to Carmarthen he had called in at the shop of a silversmith he had known for a number of years. 'I'm surprised at you, Sir Edward,' the silversmith said to him. 'You must see the man is guilty.'

'Nothing of the sort,' Sir Edward said. 'The man's innocent, and I shall prove it.'

'If you do, I'll give you this eighteenth-century silver tankard,' the silversmith said.

Some time after the trial he received a parcel which turned out to be from the silversmith. The parcel

contained the silver tankard which had been inscribed:
'I dared you to do it, and you did it.' What made the
tankard a cherished piece was that by a remarkable
coincidence it turned out to have once belonged to
Marshall Hall's grandfather, and bore his name.

THE BODY IN THE BASEMENT

Dr Hawley Harvey Crippen (1910)

Whenever a writer has dealt with the case of Dr Crippen, the story has always been tinged with some sympathy for this seemingly inoffensive little man, who is invariably portrayed as the long-suffering husband of a zero-rated music hall artiste who called herself Belle Elmore, and was bleeding him dry when he met and fell in love with Ethel Le Neve.

This myth of a gentle doctor who killed for love has been perpetuated in books, on the stage and in films, and even in the musical *Belle, or The Ballad of Dr. Crippen*, written by Wolf Mankowitz, with music by Monty Norman, and staged in London in 1961 with George Benson as Dr Crippen. I had the pleasure of seeing the show during its pre-London run in Brighton, and remember it as a tuneful musical with melodies that evoked the old music hall days. It failed at the box office, mainly because of an attack made on it by the writer Ursula Bloom who wrote an article in the *Sunday Despatch*, saying that as Ethel Le Neve was still alive, it should never have been put on.

In a sense, Ursula Bloom was right, but not for the reason she stated. What *The Ballad of Dr. Crippen* did, putting aside possibly hurting Ethel Le Neve's feelings, was to keep alive the idea that Crippen was basically a nice man.

The facts about Crippen are somewhat different.

When Crippen poisoned his wife and then cut her body to pieces like so much meat on the butcher's block before stuffing the remains under the floor of the cellar of his home at 39 Hilldrop Crescent, Holloway, North

London, he showed what could only have been an icy resolution that fits ill with the usual picture we get of him as a slightly pathetic man who had become the helpless victim of his passion for Ethel Le Neve. To kill and then dissect someone you had once loved calls for a degree of inhumanity that is generally found only in psychopaths.

No one can be sure of what fate and the future may have in store for them, least of all for someone like Hawley Harvey Crippen who was born in Coldwater, Michigan, in 1862. By the time he was twenty-one, he had decided that he would like to enter the medical profession, and as Coldwater was very much a hick town, with a population of less than 5,000 in those days, he left it as soon as he could and went to New York where he took his degree as an ear and eye specialist before joining the staff of the city's Ophthalmic Hospital. He then practised in various cities until 1887, when he met and married an Irish Catholic girl named Charlotte Bell who bore him a son they named Otto. At this period in his career, his life seemed to be on course to become financially comfortable, if uneventful, with no major ups and downs in it to disturb the even tenor of his progress.

He was living and practising in Salt Lake City when his wife suddenly died of apoplexy. Her passing was not unduly mourned by Crippen, as his wife had tended to put the shutters up where sex was concerned soon after they were married, a state of affairs that had not made the marriage a particularly happy one.

Although Crippen did not appear sexually attractive,

this did not stop him from having strong sexual desires, whetted by having had them kept in cold storage for so long. He was therefore ripe for the picking when he met Cora Turner, a slightly overblown nineteen-year-old Polish girl whose real name was Kunigunde Mackamotzki, which she had changed to her present one as she had aspirations to be a singer, and somehow did not see her real name in lights, or tripping lightly off the tongue.

Crippen met her in the same year as his wife had died, but by then he was living and practising in Brooklyn, where Cora had come to see him as a patient. As soon as he saw her he knew that she was the woman for him – as he was to feel the same way about Ethel Le Neve when she first crossed his path in 1907.

When Cora met Crippen she was already the mistress of a married man who had set her up in a flat and was also paying for singing lessons. Her present lover was a stove manufacturer, whereas Crippen was a doctor, a man in a highly respected profession, who was, moreover, willing to make her his wife. As far as Cora was concerned, there was no doubt in her mind as to where her choice lay.

The lover was quickly sent on his way, and Crippen then underwent such a barrage of sexual activity, with Cora playing the leading role, that he must have found a great difference from when he was 'enjoying' the occasional privileges that had reluctantly been allowed him by his first wife. The thought of having on permanent tap the enthusiastic services of such a woman was too much for the doctor, who bustled her to the altar on 1st September 1892.

The years rolled by, with Cora still hoping the time would come when she would become one of the singers at the Metropolitan Opera House, a piece of woeful self-miscasting by someone who should have settled for being a soprano in the local church choir.

In 1900, Crippen brought his wife to England, where he had managed to land a job as the manager of the London branch of the American-based company of Manyon's Homeopathic Remedies. Although the marriage was by no means one in which all passion was spent, it had certainly settled down to something more prosaic, with bills, rather than the peaks of ecstasy, being the main concern in Crippen's life, thanks to his wife's habit of buying herself expensive gowns and jewellery for the time when she would at last tread the boards.

As for Cora, she had at long last abandoned any thought of a career in grand opera, and had decided instead to try her luck as a musical hall artiste, and now called herself Belle Elmore for professional purposes.

In 1905, Crippen and his wife moved from their rooms in Shore Street, Bloomsbury, to 39 Hilldrop Crescent. The move took place soon after Crippen had changed jobs to work with the Drouet Institute for the Deaf, run by an unscrupulous crook who played on the gullibility of the public by promoting a whole host of worthless remedies that Crippen had been happy to actively support – in fact he was to bring out one of his own in 1908 which was called Ohrsorb, a so-called 'wonder cure' for deafness. Having entered the world of quackery, Crippen was quite content to throw aside medical ethics in favour of making an easy living.

Now back with his old firm of Manyon's with Ethel Le Neve working for him as a book-keeper and secretary, Crippen patiently tried to promote his wife's music hall career in the same way he had taken over her singing lessons in New York, and with the same lack of success, though on this occasion she did manage to get a few engagements at some of the lesser-known music halls. To supplement their income Mrs Crippen took in boarders in what seemed to her a most satisfactory arrangement: she took all the rent money for herself while Crippen still paid all the household bills.

The lodgers did not last for long, as looking after them involved a lot of drudgery that interfered with Mrs Crippen's music hall career. Once they were all out of the house Mrs Crippen became a member of the Music Hall Ladies' Guild, and eventually became its honorary treasurer. Cosy tea parties were held at Hilldrop Crescent, where such famous artistes as Marie Lloyd were in the habit of turning up, much to the delight of Mrs Crippen, who was convinced that cultivating such people would advance her career. If she did generate any goodwill in that direction, which is doubtful, she undid it all during the music hall strike of 1907, when she became a blackleg and crossed the picket line when offered the chance of appearing at the Bedford in Camden Town.

'Belle, stay out and help your own people,' shouted one of her friends.

'Don't be daft,' called out Marie Lloyd, who was also there. 'Let her in and she'll empty the house.' The remark says much for Belle's standing among her fellow artistes.

Her subsequent appearance at the Euston Palace, when she was hissed off the stage, was the nadir of her career as a music hall artiste. The incident did nothing for her temper, which was always uncertain at the best of times. As usual, Crippen bore the brunt of her bad moods, which made him turn more and more to Ethel Le Neve, with whom he had already started an affair, and who was always more than willing to offer him a pair of comforting and loving arms, if not her body, Ethel's morality being such that she was not so much concerned with sinning in the eyes of God, as to what the neighbours might think if they found out.

The situation did not come to a head until 1910, when Mrs Crippen found out about her husband and Ethel Le Neve. She had had more than one affair herself since she had been with Crippen, but this did not stop her from making a scene and threatening to leave him, taking the £600 they had in their joint account with her. This nasty moment came at a bad time financially for Crippen as his wife had been letting his money run through her fingers like water, making him spend it on expensive suppers at the Savoy or the Trocadero, or on entertaining her raffish friends at home. On top of it all, he was now working on a commission-only basis for his firm.

If every husband who killed his wife did so because she had threatened to leave him and take off with their joint savings, the law courts would be full of men having to face up to the consequences of their crimes. Crippen's motives for killing his wife, therefore, seem difficult to fathom, although several theories have been put forward over the years. More likely than not he had simply become tired of living at Hilldrop Crescent with his now blowsy wife who had insisted on doing out the house in pink throughout, even down to tying pink velvet bows to the corners of the pictures on the wall – an act of execrable taste that some might think was motive enough for murder.

Whatever the reason, Crippen celebrated the New Year by going out and ordering five grains of hyoscine, for which he signed the poison book, telling the chemist that it was for certain preparations made by Manyon's. By 19th January, Crippen had five grains of hyoscine in the house. He then suggested to his wife that they throw a dinner party for the Martinettis, a couple of music hall artistes who seemed to be two of his wife's special friends. The dinner party was arranged for the 31st January, and when the guests arrived that evening, they were surprised to find Crippen so eager to show the Martinettis that there was nothing amiss in his relationship with his wife. When they left that evening, the last mental picture they carried away with them was of Mrs Crippen standing on the doorstep waving them goodbye. It was the last time they were ever to see her.

It is impossible to say exactly when Crippen murdered his wife, but it is more than probable that he killed her the morning after the dinner party, when he put hyoscine in her coffee and then dragged the body into the bathroom where he calmly dissected it, using the tap water to run away the blood. The limbs and certain organs were probably burnt in the grate, while what was left of poor Mrs Crippen after that was taken down to the cellar and buried beneath the brick flooring.

As it must have taken several days before the job was completed, one doesn't need to have a great deal of imagination to visualize something of the horrors that Crippen left behind him in the house when he interrupted his labours to go to work – that is when he was not busy pawning some of his wife's jewellery, which we know he started to do on 2nd February.

It needs a certain type of mind to plan and execute a hideous crime of this nature, plus an iron stamina to carry out such a task without running screaming out of the house. Crippen, however, was more than equal to the occasion. Not only did he commit this grisly murder, but he also laid down the groundwork for its concealment without once faltering in his purpose. The tissue of lies that he gave out to explain his wife's sudden absence from the scene had been carefully thought out beforehand, and only foundered when his wife's friendships with her music hall cronies proved to be more durable than he had realized. Instead of taking his statements at their face value, they approached the police.

On 2nd February, as well as pawning one of his wife's rings, and a pair of her earrings, for which he received £80, he wrote to the Music Hall Ladies' Guild informing them that his wife had suddenly left for America and would be away for some time, and he was therefore tendering her resignation on her behalf. The members were surprised and a little disappointed with the news as Mrs Crippen had been well liked, though she was considered something of a joke as a music hall artiste.

Despite her one lapse in crossing the picket line, they had given her a silver bracelet in appreciation of her work for the Guild, which was essentially a charitable organization. Their liking for Mrs Crippen, incidentally, had not extended to Mr Crippen, for whom they had little time, and who had been nick-named 'the half crown king' by Marie Lloyd, due to his habit of fumbling in his pocket when it came to be his turn to buy a drink, and then apologetically saying that he had left his money at home and could someone please lend him half a crown, which Crippen never paid back.

On February 20th, Crippen wrote to the Martinettis informing them that he had just learned from his wife that she was seriously ill with pleuro-pneumonia. This was stage two in Crippen's scheme to remove Mrs Crippen's name from the social scene.

Stage three followed on the 24th February when Mrs Martinetti received a telegram informing her that Mrs Crippen had died suddenly. This was followed by a small flood of memorial cards and an announcement of his wife's death in *The Era*.

By then Ethel had overcome her reluctance about sleeping with Crippen, and they had been in the habit of going to one of the sleazy hotels in the Paddington area, a routine that Ethel had come to dislike. It was perhaps for this reason that on 12th March Crippen made the mistake of bringing her to live openly with him at Hilldrop Crescent. He had already caused tongues to wag when he had taken her to a dinner and ball held to raise money for the Music Hall Benevolent Fund. It was bad enough that Crippen should be seen with another woman, but what really put the cat among the pigeons was when Ethel was seen to be wearing a very distinctive brooch that was recognized by some as being a piece of Mrs Crippen's jewellery. Knowing her well enough to be aware that she would never have gone away without taking her jewellery with her, the members of the Guild who were present began to have their first doubts about the truth of Crippen's statement that she had died in America. When it became common knowledge that Ethel was now living with Crippen at Hilldrop Crescent they became suspicious enough to bring the matter to the attention of Scotland Yard.

The man Scotland Yard put on the case was Inspector Dew, who visited Crippen in his office in the company of Sergeant Mitchell. Knowing that his story about his wife would never stand up to the polite but insistent questioning on the part of Inspector Dew, Crippen was astute enough to change his story almost immediately.

'I'm afraid the story I put about concerning my wife was a lie,' he said frankly. 'The truth of the matter is that my wife and I quarrelled, and she ran off with one of her previous lovers to America. As far as I know she is safe and well and living somewhere over there. I made the story up to silence the gossipmongers, and to avoid any scandal.' He smiled wanly. 'I'm afraid it is all rather embarrassing.'

The Inspector accepted the story without comment. 'I'm afraid we shall have to find Mrs Crippen somehow. In the meantime I would like to look over your house if I may.'

'Of course,' Crippen assented.

He met the two policemen at Hilldrop Crescent when Ethel was out and stood by while they searched the house from top to bottom. Their search produced nothing that was of any use to them, and they left, promising to keep in touch.

It was at this point that Crippen seems to have suddenly lost his nerve. He had all but convinced Inspector Dew that he was innocent, and all he needed to do was to sit tight with Ethel at Hilldrop Crescent while the police sought in vain for his wife in America. In the due course of time he could have quietly married Ethel and then given up his tenancy of the house and moved, probably to America, where he could have lived out the rest of his life in peace. Instead, he fled with Ethel to Antwerp, leaving the house to be explored again by Inspector Dew when he called, only to find it no longer occupied. What makes Crippen's behaviour even more strange was that he did not depart in panic-stricken flight, but first paid all the household bills and generally put his affairs in order before departing, taking with him only the minimum amount of luggage.

When Inspector Dew called at the house that day and found it unoccupied, he immediately became suspicious and searched it again. It took him three days of painstaking searching before he found at last the mouldering remains of Mrs Crippen under the cellar floor. A warrant for the arrest of Crippen and Ethel Le Neve was issued on 16th July, and a description of Crippen circulated throughout the country. If anything, the description flattered him, and was to lead to the near arrest of a number of innocent people, including one man who was pulled in twice, much to his annoyance and to the embarrassment of Inspector Dew who had come in for a certain amount of criticism from the press for allowing Crippen and Ethel Le Neve to slip through his fingers when he had already been informed that Crippen might have murdered his wife. The escape was given an enormous amount of coverage by the news-papers, including the *Daily Mail*, which offered £100 to anyone who could supply information leading to the whereabouts of the missing couple. By then, however, Crippen and his companion were safely in Bruges, with Ethel now dressed, rather unconvincingly, as a boy and posing as the son of Mr Robinson, as Crippen was calling himself.

On 20th July, Mr Robinson and Master Robinson boarded the SS *Montrose*, sailing out of Antwerp and bound for Canada and America. It was an extraordinary situation, with the two lovers fleeing across the ocean with one of them dressed as a boy, and it did much to invest the story with an aura of glamour that it did not merit when the public became aware of the circum-stances of their attempted escape.

It is possible that having got that far, Crippen and Ethel might have escaped if it had not been for the alertness of Captain Kendell, who noticed on the ship's second day out of port that Master Robinson's trousers were extremely tight around the hips for someone who was supposed to be a boy. He noticed, furthermore, that Master Robinson's hat was padded with paper to make it fit. Already suspicious that the two were the couple he had read about in the newspapers, the clincher for

Captain Kendell came when he saw the two of them holding hands like lovers. He immediately sent a wireless message to the Liverpool police, who passed on the message to Scotland Yard, where Inspector Dew had been driven almost out of his mind chasing up all the reported sightings of Crippen and Ethel, only to find himself interviewing each time someone who bore only a faint resemblance to Crippen. When he was informed of this new lead, Dew had an instinctive feeling that this time he really was on the verge of capturing Crippen and his companion – providing of course that he could approach them before they left the ship in Canada. After obtaining permission to undertake the journey from the Assistant Commissioner, Sir Melville Macnaughten, Dew booked a passage on the *Laurentic*, a faster ship than the *Montrose*, and one that should get him into Quebec before Crippen and Ethel.

Inspector Dew did not catch up with the *Montrose* until it was in Canadian waters, where he boarded the ship off Father Point disguised as a pilot and accompanied by a Chief Inspector of the Canadian police, posing as a ship's navigator. Together with Captain Kendell, the three men approached Crippen, who was enjoying a quiet stroll on the deck.

'Good morning, Dr Crippen. I believe you know me,' Inspector Dew said dryly. 'I am arresting you for the murder and mutilation of your wife, Cora Crippen, in London on or about 1st February last.'

Crippen took the news calmly. 'I am not sorry,' he said. 'The anxiety has been too much.' He then spoke of Ethel. 'It is only fair to say that she knew nothing about it. I never told her anything.' Ethel was arrested a few minutes later in her cabin, where she was reading a book when Inspector Dew entered. Unlike Crippen, she did not react to the sight of Inspector Dew with the same calmness. Instead, she let out a loud scream and fainted.

It is worth pausing at this point to try and answer the question that must be in the reader's mind. Did Ethel know when she fled with Crippen abroad that he had murdered his wife? From much of the evidence it seems extremely unlikely. Crippen had told her, as he had done everyone else, that his wife had died in America. From then on the sequence of events must have seemed quite logical to her. The gift of Mrs Crippen's jewellery, his flaunting of her before his wife's friends at the dinner and ball, and her installation in the house at Hilldrop Crescent, was to her the long overdue recognition of someone who had at last assumed her rightful place at the side of the man she loved.

Ethel is known to have detested 39 Hilldrop Crescent from the moment she had stepped inside the house, and she was therefore only too happy to go along with his suggestion that they move as soon as possible, taking nothing with them. 'To make a new life with no memories of Cora around us to mar our happiness', as Crippen might well have put it.

The only sticking point in this attempt to prove that Ethel knew nothing of the murder is, how then did he manage to persuade her to have her hair cropped and to dress up as a boy? To find a possible answer it is necessary to take a quantum leap into an area of pure speculation based on what we know about Ethel as a person, accepting as a fact that the dressing up took place abroad when Crippen, who knew French, learned from the newspapers that the police were after him. At this point he probably told her that his wife had run off with another man and that the police wrongly suspected him of murder. Ethel never once doubted at this stage that he was anything but innocent. She was a simple, uncomplicated girl, with a liking for romantic novels like *Audrey's Recompense*, a popular romance written by Mrs Georgie Sheldon, which she was reading at the time of her arrest. Crippen's suggestion that she should pose as a boy therefore took on the aspect of a romantic adventure story with herself as its leading character. Reality did not intrude until Inspector Dew entered her cabin. Even then, it was only when she stood side by side with Crippen in the dock that the chilling truth was brought home to her that he had actually murdered his wife. The wonder of it all is that she continued to love him to the end of her days.

Crippen and Ethel were taken to Quebec, and after the extradition proceedings were completed, they were taken back to England, where their ship docked at Liverpool on 28th August. After a brief appearance at Bow Street, they were committed for trial at the Old Bailey.

When Crippen and Ethel Le Neve took their places in the dock on the morning of 28th October, everyone who was conversant with the details of the case knew that Crippen, at least, had very little chance of being acquitted. If he had been represented by Marshall Hall, who was noted for his ability to make a case for an accused whose chances of acquittal had seemed slim, the outcome of Crippen's trial could well have been different. In fact, Hall was always convinced that he could have got him off with a sentence for manslaughter. Instead, Crippen had the relatively inexperienced Alfred Tobin, KC, who was to show himself as being no match for Richard Muir, who was appearing for the prosecution, and was known to be deadly in examination. Ethel Le Neve was to be better served by Frederick Edwin Smith acting as her defence lawyer.

A hushed silence fell over the crowded court when Lord Alverstone, the Lord Chief Justice, came in and took his seat before the court over which he was to preside for the next five days. The case that followed was one that had long and boring stretches as the defence and prosecution argued over the medical evidence in which it was established that Mrs Crippen had been given hyoscine before she had been dissected and her remains buried beneath the floor of the cellar at 39 Hilldrop Crescent. One of the highlights of the case was when Muir revealed that the remains had been wrapped up in a pair of pyjamas that Crippen had bought from Jones Brothers of Holloway.

'Who was missing? Whose remains could be buried in them?' Muir demanded. 'Nobody but Belle Elmore.'

This might have made a fine dramatic moment in court if it had not already been proven that the disinterred remains were those of Mrs Crippen, when a soup plate had been passed round the jury, containing fragments of flesh bearing scar tissue consistent with that of an operation that Mrs Crippen had undergone before their marriage.

The real highlight of the trial came on the fourth day when Crippen faced Muir from the dock. His manner remained calm throughout Muir's relentless questioning, but by the time the prosecutor had finished, it was obvious that the jury would bring in no other verdict than that of guilty. True enough, within twenty-five minutes they had returned with a verdict everyone had been expecting, and Crippen was sentenced by Lord Alverstone to be hanged at Pentonville Prison.

With Ethel Le Neve, the case for the defence was much more straightforward, and was one in which Frederick Smith openly challenged the prosecution to prove that she was anything other than innocent of the crime for which she was being charged – that of being an accessory after the fact to the murder. This time Muir was not out for a 'kill', and allowed Smith to carry most of the day, with the result that Ethel Le Neve was found innocent and allowed to leave the court.

After he had been found guilty, Crippen wrote a number of rather touching letters to Ethel from the condemned cell, which proved beyond doubt that he was genuinely in love with her, though with an intensity that bordered on the pathological. She in turn wrote back regularly and visited him on several occasions. To his credit, his only thoughts in prison seemed to be of Ethel's future welfare. When his appeal was turned down, Crippen accepted his fate with resignation, and his last days before he went to the scaffold were spent in writing to Ethel, who was preparing to leave the country and make a new life for herself in America. At his own request a photograph of Ethel was placed in his coffin.

What is there about this case which has always made it so fascinating to the public and has made it one of the classic murder cases of the 20th century? Crippen was not the first, nor the last man to have murdered his wife and then buried her in the cellar of his house. Nor were *crimes passionnels* unknown in this country. One of the most obvious reasons, of course, is that it was the first time that the newfangled invention of the wireless was used to catch someone on the run from the police. Secondly, it was the physical appearance of Crippen, whose gentle and mild manner made it seem almost impossible that he should be capable of murdering his wife in the manner he did. Lastly, the murder had been carried out against the background of a genuine love affair between two people which lifted it out of the mire into something more than a squalid case in which Crippen received in the end only what he deserved.

The story of Dr Crippen and Ethel Le Neve is one in which one can only feel rather sorry for Ethel, who eventually came back to this country and married. If one is tempted to feel the same about Crippen, it might be a salutary exercise to conjure up a picture of him at 39 Hilldrop Cresent, methodically hacking Mrs Crippen to pieces, while standing stark naked to avoid her blood splashing on to his clothes.

If anyone is interested in reading more on this case, I would particularly recommend, out of all the books and articles that have been written on Crippen, Tom Cullen's *Crippen: The Mild Mannered Murderer*, published by the Bodley Head in 1967, which has been a valuable source book for writers on the case, myself included, ever since it was published.

A LONG TRAIL OF DEATH

Mary Ann Cotton (1873)

Mary Ann Cotton was a quiet, unassuming woman who would not have attracted a second glance in the street, and wherever she had lived her neighbours had always spoken well of her and knew her as a God-fearing chapelgoer and a law-abiding citizen. This was the image she gave to everyone, but in reality she was a monster in human form, who is today considered as being Britain's greatest mass murderer, with an impressive murder count of no less than sixteen victims – including most of her children. There may have been more.

During her trial, a newspaper artist drew a picture of her in which he depicted her as being a cruel-looking, cold-eyed woman with high cheekbones and sensuous lips, whereas she was a gentle-looking creature, if the photograph that was taken when she was in prison is anything to go by. The artist can be forgiven for drawing an entirely false portrait of her; in common with all newspaper artists who were sent to cover a trial, his brief would have been to show the prisoner in the dock looking as if she might well be a murderess. As it happened, the artist had inadvertently captured the real woman behind the mask.

The saga of her unholy progress through life to the gallows began in 1832, when she was born Mary Ann Robson in the mining village of Low Moorsley in Co. Durham. Soon after she was born the family moved to East Rainton, where she grew up in the tightly knit mining community where the family lived in a small two-bedroomed cottage supplied by the owners of the

Hazard pit where her father worked as a pitman. Like most mining cottages in those days it was woefully short of the amenities one would expect to find today in even the most humble abode – the lavatory, for instance, being nothing more than a hole in the ground outside, housed in a hut.

After moving with her parents to the nearby village of Murton, where Mary Ann became a regular chapelgoer, life went on very much as usual until her father was killed when he fell down a pit shaft in 1842. When her mother remarried, Mary Ann worked for a while as a nursemaid, and then as a dressmaker, until she met William Mowbray, whom she married in 1854. As he was a common labourer at the time she met him, it was hardly a step up in the world for her, and for a while she was forced to move frequently to wherever her husband could get casual work until he was finally able to get regular work in Penzance with a railway construction company.

They eventually returned to Murton, and Mary Ann brought with her a newly born child. There had been three other children, but they had died, she informed all her old friends. If they thought she seemed to be bearing up remarkably well in the circumstances, they said nothing.

There is no evidence to suggest that she had murdered those three children, so if we give Mary Ann the benefit of the doubt, her murderous activities did not begin until she had returned to Murton, where she had another child who died soon afterwards from gastric fever, an illness that was to figure large in Mary Ann's infamous progress to the gallows.

From then onwards, until the family finally settled in
Sunderland after living for a brief spell in South Hatton,
she had had four more children, and two of these had died
from 'gastric fever' as well as the child who had been born
in Penzance. In 1865, after having a remarkably long run
for his money, Mowbray was suddenly taken ill and was
carried off with the same illness, leaving Mary Ann better
off by £35 insurance money, and free to marry again. She
was then thirty-two and alone, except for the two surviving children. One of them she disposed of in her usual way,
while the other, named Isabella, was taken in by Mary
Ann's mother. She then went to work in the Sunderland
Fever Hospital, where she met George Ward while he was
a patient there. When she married him in the August of the
same year as her husband's death, she probably thought
she had taken a step up in the world as Ward was an engineer by profession, and a strong, virile-looking man, who
looked as if he would be a good bed companion. What she
had not allowed for was that the fever that had laid him
low had sapped his strength and made him unfit to work.
She had hardly settled in the house with Ward than she
suddenly found herself saddled with a man who was now
on parish relief and bringing in a mere four shillings a
week instead of the reasonable income she had expected
from a man who was a skilled engineer. As far as Mary
Ann was concerned, he was now a liability and someone
she wanted to be rid of as soon as possible. He died fourteen months after they were married, after a long and
lingering illness with symptoms that included paralysis of
his hands and feet.

Once she had buried Ward, Mary Ann looked around

for a job and found one as a housekeeper to a local
shipwright named John Robinson, whose wife had just
died, leaving him with five children to bring up. No one
seeing her enter Robinson's house for the first time
could have seen this poorly but neatly dressed little
woman as a harbinger of death who was to wipe out
most of that household before she blithely went on her
way, continuing to leave a trail of death in her wake
before the police finally came to take her away.

Unaware of the monster he had brought into the
house, John Robinson was infatuated with her from the
start and quickly made her his mistress. No sooner were
her feet under the table, so to speak, than Mary Ann set
about decimating the household. Within weeks of her
arrival, Robinson's ten-month-old son was suddenly
taken ill and died, and no sooner was he buried than two
more of the children had died. These deaths occurred in
the Spring of 1867 and by then she had also murdered
her mother, after visiting her while she lay ill in bed.
Being a woman who did not like to see things going to
waste, Mary Ann went off with the bed linen and some
of her mother's clothing as soon as she was dead, openly
departing with them under the shocked gaze of the
neighbours. With her mother gone, it was inevitable that
Mary Ann's daughter Isabella should be the next to go
now that there was no one to look after her. She was
taken into Robinson's home, where she died soon
afterwards.

In the November of the same year, Mary Ann bore
Robinson a girl who was dead by the March of the
following year. All the deaths that had occurred while

she was with Robinson were put down to gastric fever.

One may well ask how it was that Mary Ann managed to get away with it all this time, with the deceased readily given death certificates in which the cause of death was invariably given as gastric fever, a complaint whose symptoms were not unlike those of someone who had been given arsenic. It was not as incredible as it might seem. To begin with, the nineteenth century was an age when hygiene was almost non-existent, and people who lived in humble circumstances lived in rat-infested houses where food that was suspect to begin with was left exposed to rodents and flies. As a result, people who lived in that strata of society succumbed to all manner of then unknown diseases. These were conveniently diagnosed as gastric fever by overworked doctors who were not looking for a case of arsenical poisoning in a patient who had just died in poverty-stricken circumstances, leaving no money to be inherited, and therefore providing no motive for murder. It was this apparent lack of motive that allowed Mary Ann to get away with murder for twenty years before she was finally arrested.

The only persons who suspected all was not well were Robinson's three sisters, who had taken an instant dislike to her and did their best to dissuade him from marrying her. He ignored their warnings and married her in 1867 and soon afterwards she had a second child by him.

One would have thought that at this stage Mary Ann would have stopped killing with such abandon. By her standards she was now well-off and living with a man who had money in the bank and seemed genuinely fond of her. She rewarded him by planning to poison him almost from the moment she entered the house. There was only one snag. To make it worthwhile she had to persuade him to take out an insurance on his life, and this was something that Robinson refused to do. When she saw he had no intention of changing his mind, she then tried to take out an insurance on his life herself, only to be found out by her husband, who put a stop to the idea before she could even make the first payment.

Instead of poisoning him anyway, just to keep her hand in, she left him, and shortly afterwards picked up with a sailor who lived with her for a while before stealing the few personal possessions she had and disappearing, never to be seen again. He was lucky. If he had stayed with her, he would probably have been added to Mary Ann's ever-growing list of victims.

This was a further setback for Mary Ann, who had left Robinson for no other reason than that he had refused to fall in with her plans to poison him, only to be robbed and deserted by another man. Her spirits must therefore have been at a low ebb when she had the good fortune to meet Margaret Cotton, whom she had not seen for many years. Margaret introduced Mary Ann to her brother, Frederick, who had recently lost his wife and two of his four children who had died from natural causes, leaving a four-year-old son named Charles Edward, and another boy named Frederick, to bring up. Lonely and unable to cope with the situation, Frederick Cotton was a natural prey for Mary Ann, who immediately made it obvious that she was available if he

wanted her; she omitted to tell him that she was still
legally married to Robinson. They became lovers and
were bigamously married in 1870, but not before
Margaret Cotton had suddenly died in what can only be
described as suspicious circumstances, having passed
away after a bout of violent stomach pains. With a little
more imagination than usual the doctor had diagnosed
her death as being caused by pleuro-pneumonia. Clearly
Mary Ann had an eye to the future when she poisoned
her sister-in-law, as she undoubtedly did. As she had
already earmarked Frederick for death in the not too
distant future, she was probably making sure that
Margaret would not be around to inherit any of his
money.

Mary Ann was now pregnant again when the couple
went to live in West Auckland in Co. Durham. Either by
chance or design on Mary Ann's part, they moved to a
house in Johnson Terrace, where one of her old lovers,
a coal miner named George Natress, was also living.
Once she knew that Natress would be happy to marry
her if Frederick died, her husband's already impending
death was hurried forward, and two months after they
had moved to Johnson Terrace, he was dead of gastric
fever. After a respectable period of mourning, Natress
moved in, ostensibly as her lodger.

At that point in time, Natress was under the im-
pression that they would soon be married, but by then
Mary Ann had already met an excise officer named
Quick-Manning and was having an affair with him.
There is no telling how long Natress would have lasted
if Quick-Manning had not arrived on the scene. As it

was, Mary Ann now found herself in something of a quandary. Either she stayed with Natress and saw how events shaped out with him, or she got rid of him and made a bid to get Quick-Manning – a man who was higher up the social scale than anyone she had ever met before. As far as she was concerned it was no choice at all, and Natress went the way of all her other victims before he had hardly settled in the house.

When she found out that she was already pregnant by Quick-Manning, Mary Ann decided the time had come for her to embark on a poisoning spree. Cotton's son, her own child, and the baby she had just had by Cotton were all poisoned and buried within the space of a month without a single eyebrow being raised as the coffins were taken out of the house. Even Quick-Manning made no comment, but then why should he when, as late as 1844, a newborn child of the working classes in the provinces had just one chance in two of reaching the age of five.

Only one hindrance now stood in the way before she married Quick-Manning, and that was Cotton's surviving son, Charles Edward, who had only been spared so far because she had been too busy poisoning the rest of the household to have the time to deal with him. In a rare softhearted moment, she first tried to get him put in the workhouse, trying to enlist the aid of Thomas Riley, who ran the corner general shop, and was also a public relief officer.

'Times are very hard since my husband has gone,' she told him, 'and the boy is preventing me from taking a lodger.'

Knowing that she was having an affair with Quick-Manning, which had by now become common knowledge in the street, Riley ignored her plea for help with the boy, figuring that Quick-Manning was likely to marry her shortly, putting an end to any current financial problems.

A week later he happened to be passing her house when he saw Mary Ann standing on her doorstep with tears in her eyes. 'My boy is dead,' she told him.

As he had seen the boy less than a week earlier, when he seemed in perfect health, Riley became suspicious, especially when he remembered how the three other children had died, one after the other within a month. He went to the police, and then to Dr Kilburn, the local GP.

'I know the boy had been ill with gastro-enteritis. In fact, my assistant, Dr Chalmers, called three times in the week, as I did myself only yesterday,' Dr Kilburn told him.

The doctor thought about the matter for a few moments. 'In the circumstances, I shall withhold the usual death certificate and ask for permission to carry out a postmortem,' he told Riley. He sighed. 'This is a bad business, Mr Riley. If your suspicions prove to be correct, a lot of people are not going to believe it. She has always been well thought of round here. There has also been much sympathy for her misfortunes, and there has even been talk of making a collection for her.'

The first intimation Mary Ann had that for once everything was not going to plan, was when the local insurance man told her that he could not hand over the insurance money without first seeing the death certificate.

'I shall get one from Dr Kilburn,' Mary Ann told him confidently.

Even after Dr Kilburn had refused to give her the certificate, it did not dawn on her that she was in serious trouble until the coroner asked her to attend the inquest that was being held the very next day at the Rose and Crown, next to her house. As luck would have it, the coroner had acted too quickly, and Dr Kilburn had a bare hour in which to conduct his postmortem before the inquest was held. The result was that in the short time available to him, he had been unable to find anything that might indicate that the boy had died of anything but natural causes. When the jury brought in a verdict to that effect, Riley was still convinced that she had poisoned the boy. Outside the Rose and Crown he encountered Mary Ann, who railed against him bitterly.

'This is all your doing,' she shouted. 'You have tried to bring shame on an innocent woman, and you have failed, thank the Lord.'

'I still think you murdered the boy,' Riley said coldly, as he walked away.

Inevitably, there was a great deal of gossip in the village, and people began to avoid Mary Ann, including Quick-Manning, although she was carrying his child. Now practically destitute, and with no help from Quick-Manning, Mary Ann made it clear that she could not afford to pay for Charles Edward to be buried, and he was placed in a pauper's grave.

By then Mary Ann must have thought she was in the clear, but she had not reckoned with Dr Kilburn, who had left the Rose and Crown feeling that he had been made to look something of a fool for having supported Riley without any evidence to prove that Mary Ann had killed her stepson. Like Riley, he was now convinced that she had poisoned him, and was determined not to let the matter rest. Fortunately, he had kept most of the contents of the body, and he now examined them at leisure. This time he found enough arsenic to send him scurrying off to see the local police superintendent.

The following morning the superintendent, accompanied by two sergeants, arrived at Mary Ann's house with a warrant for her arrest for the murder of Charles Edward Cotton. She was led away and taken to Bishop Auckland and placed in a cell where she languished for more than a month before she was brought up before the magistrates and committed for trial at the Durham Assizes.

During that period, the bodies of Charles Edward, Natress, Cotton's son Frederick, and Mary Ann's eighteen-month-old son were all exhumed. In all the bodies enough arsenic had been found to make it almost certain that she would be meeting the hangman in a very short space of time.

It is worthwhile at this point to try and find the answers to two questions. Firstly, how had someone like Mary Ann been able to acquire the medical knowledge to enable her to murder so many people without being detected when she was hardly able to put together a letter, let alone read a book on poisons? Her knowledge came from being a housewife who knew that soft soap was mixed with arsenic in order to remove bed bugs, and was readily available from any chemist, as were arsenic-

impregnated flypapers. The other question that automat-
ically comes to mind when reading her case is: why did
she commit murder time after time? It has been said that
she did it mostly for the insurance money, but not all her
victims were insured, and when they were, the amounts
she received were hardly worth the risk.

It has also been said that sex was one of the driving
forces behind the murders, that no sooner had she found
one man than she wanted another. Certainly, she seemed
to have had a busy sex life, if the number of children she
had are any guide. But this does not explain how she
could kill off nearly all her children without a qualm.
The truth of the matter, one suspects, was that she was
indeed a hot-blooded woman, but one who was in-
capable of feeling anything for anybody, except for the
fleeting excitement that her lovers gave her in bed. She
did not kill them for love, or primarily for money, but
mostly because those around her had suddenly become
a hindrance to her plans for the future, however modest
they might be. She was a cold, cruel and heartless
creature who had blotted out lives without the slightest
compunction. But even so, not even she deserved the
terrible manner of her death.

Mary Ann Cotton came to trial in the March of 1873.
Leading for the prosecution was Charles Russell (later
Lord Russell) who was to add to his substantial reputation by his stirring defence of Mrs Maybrick in 1889,
while the defence was carried out by Thomas Campbell
Foster, a Leeds lawyer who had been approached by the
court because Mary Ann had no money to pay for her
defence. She was lucky. Foster was an experienced and

capable lawyer with considerable courtroom expertise; not that he could help much in a case such as hers, where the evidence of guilt was so overwhelming.

One by one, the prosecution paraded its witnesses before the jury, and each one of them added one more nail in Mary Ann's coffin. There was the testimony of a neighbour named Mary Dodds, who told the court that Mary Ann had asked her to buy a mixture of soft soap and arsenic from the local chemist as she needed it to remove bugs from the woodwork of one of her beds, and there was the corroborative evidence of the chemist who had made an entry in his notebook to the effect that he had given Miss Dodds approximately half an ounce of the deadly mixture, more than enough to kill a healthy adult, let alone a weak and sickly child. A cleaner who had worked for Mary Ann added to the hostility of the jury towards the prisoner by relating how Mary Ann had physically ill-treated the boy in her presence and had deliberately kept him in a half-starved condition. Riley also had his day in court when he related how Mary Ann had told him that the boy was in the way and preventing her from marrying Quick-Manning. The combined effect of this evidence was not conclusive in itself, but the results of the postmortems were irrefutable, though the defence did its best to throw an element of doubt over the findings by getting Dr Kilburn to admit that arsenic was sometimes found in graveyards, and could have impregnated the corpses. Seeing that the jury remained visibly unimpressed, Campbell Foster then tried another tack. Was it not possible, he argued, that the green wallpaper impregnated with arsenic in the boy's bedroom had thrown off deadly fumes and had slowly poisoned the boy? At this point, Justice Archibald interrupted him, saying that the argument for the defence was so speculative that it was hardly worth asking the question. All the defence could get out of Dr Kilburn that was of any value, was to get him to admit that the dead boy would have been susceptible to disease as he was delicate.

Campbell Foster knew full well that whatever tactics he tried would be completely negated by the evidence of the postmortems that had been carried out on the other victims who had met their fate in that house of death. He argued that the evidence relating to those deaths was inadmissible, as Mary Ann was being tried only on the death of Charles Edward. The judge overruled him and from then on the verdict was a foregone conclusion. The jury took less than an hour to bring in a verdict of guilty. The awful majesty of the law then proceeded on its inexorable course, with the judge putting on his black cap and sentencing Mary Ann to death. At those dreaded words, Mary Ann collapsed and was half carried out of the court and taken to Durham County Jail to await the carrying out of the death sentence.

When she had been awaiting trial, a baby girl by Quick-Manning had been born and she was allowed to have the child in the death cell, where it was kept in a cot. It is doubtful that she had much motherly love, though no doubt the two stone-faced police who were with her all the time tried to make up for it, thereby bringing a touch of humanity into the cheerless place, where the mother's thoughts were focused on the results of the pleas for clemency that had been sent to the Home Secretary. They were all rejected.

Her child was taken from her five days before her execution, and on 24th March 1873 she was taken to the scaffold, where William Calcraft, the executioner, awaited her.

What followed was like something out of a nightmare. Calcraft was not one of the latter-day types of executioner such as Pierpoint, who always tried to hang his victim as quickly and painlessly as possible, but a judicial murderer, whose rough and ready methods had already led to a number of distressing scenes on the scaffold. On occasion Calcraft had completely bungled the job and been forced to grab on to the legs of someone he had just hanged, before his unfortunate victim died several minutes later. On this day, he was to excel himself.

With the help of his assistant, Calcraft pinioned her arms and legs and then put the hood over her head before stepping off the trap door that was about to open and plunge Mary Ann to her death. As soon as the signal was given, the trap door swung open and she plunged into space, where she began to writhe at the end of the rope which was slowly choking her to death, instead of snapping her neck immediately. She hung there for three agonizing minutes, and then at last the twitching and writhing body was stilled, and Mary Ann was dead. Her adult life had been one of unmitigated evil, but no one deserved to die as she had done, at the hands of a callous executioner whose only interest was not how his victim died, but his fee for carrying out his obscene task.

The case of Mary Ann Cotton does not seem to have

been written up in detail, except by Arthur Appleton in his book *Mary Ann Cotton: Her Story and Trial*, published by Michael Joseph in 1973, and a very useful source book.

DEATH OF AN UNWANTED LOVER

Madeleine Smith (1857)

'I shall never give my consent for you to marry this man,' Mr Smith said. 'He is not socially acceptable to me and your mother,' he added with distaste. 'Moreover he is a *foreigner*.'

Madeleine Smith listened with dismay as her father ranted on as he paced the carpet, uttering such phrases as 'the man is a common adventurer' and 'bringing shame on the family by such a marriage'. 'I would rather see you dead in your grave than married to him,' Mr Smith concluded.

Whatever hopes that Madeleine Smith had cherished of marrying her lover, Emile L'Angelier, were gone by the time her father had finally swept out of the room with his wife following meekly behind him. Taken aback by the force of her father's objections to the marriage, she had promised never to see L'Angelier again. In this she had lied. At this stage in her life, L'Angelier was her whole being, a man to whom she had given herself freely and without regret, finding in his arms a happiness she had never thought possible until she had met him. As she had sat there, listening to her father raging on, she had decided she would continue seeing her lover behind her parents' backs, meeting him in secret. It was a cry of silent rebellion that has echoed down the ages, and never more than in the Victorian era, when Papa's ruling on all matters was absolute in the household of a middle class family.

In this case, Mr Smith was not being a domestic tyrant, riding roughshod over his daughter's feelings. He merely wanted her to make a good marriage, and Emile

L'Angelier was not the sort of man that he had
envisaged his daughter marrying. Apart from the social
implications of such a union, he had good cause to be
concerned about L'Angelier.

L'Angelier was an opportunist with his eye to the
main chance, who had seen in marrying Madeleine an
entrée into a way of life of which he had always
dreamed but had never been able to achieve, given his
background.

He was born in Jersey in the Channel Islands, the son
of French parents who ran a small market garden in the
capital town of St Helier. They had never really risen
much above their humble beginnings in France, and as
a result Emile had grown up with only the rudiments of
an education and very little in the way of expectations
in life beyond working in the family business. Seeing no
future for himself on the island, he went to Edinburgh,
where he spent the next five years working for a firm of
seed merchants. In 1847 he went to Paris, where he
joined the National Guard and fought in the revolution
of 1848. In 1852 he went back to Edinburgh, only to
drift on from there to Dundee and then to Glasgow,
where he obtained a job with Huggins and Company,
working for the princely sum of £26 a year, plus a small
living allowance, which enabled him to find lodgings. In
all he had frittered away nearly twelve years of his life
and got precisely nowhere. It is little wonder that Mr
Smith flatly refused to allow his daughter to marry him.

Although a baptized Roman Catholic, Emile knew
that his faith would not open many doors for him in a
city where the majority of people were either Presby-

terians or Protestants. He therefore joined St Jude's Episcopal Church purely as a matter of expediency.

At St Jude's he was fortunate enough to become friends with a Mary Perry. It was a strange attraction of opposites that brought them together. Sex did not come into it as Mary was a spinster with spectacles and greying hair, while L'Angelier had become something of a perfumed fop, while retaining much of that animal magnetism that had turned women's heads as a young man in his early twenties. Loneliness brought them together and was to make her his willing accomplice later on.

It was Mary Perry who drew him to the attention of the Reverend Charles Popham Miles, a kindly man who took to Emile and suggested that he should move to a more salubrious area than the one he was living in at the time. A room was found for him at the home of Peter Clark, curator of the Royal Botanic Gardens, and it was probably there that he first saw Madeleine Smith one Sunday afternoon while strolling in the gardens.

The contact that was to prove so fatal to both of them was made by a mutual friend named Robert Baird when they encountered Madeleine and her sister Bessie walking down Sauchiehall Street. Most of the eligible young bachelors in Glasgow were staid, rather stern-faced young men, and rather lacking a sense of humour. L'Angelier with his Gallic expressiveness and boulevard charm was therefore quite different to anyone she had met before. A further meeting was arranged, and from then on events proceeded rapidly, with the two of them taking unchaperoned walks together.

They began their now famous correspondence. Only a few of L'Angelier's letters survive, as Madeleine must have destroyed them rather than risk her father getting hold of them and reading L'Angelier's passionate outpourings. Nearly all her letters, on the other hand, survive, and have formed the basis of at least two books that have been written on Madeleine Smith and her trial.

Much has been said of Madeleine's good looks, but the sketches that were done of her at the time show her as a strong-faced, rather than a beautiful young lady. Not that her looks were really the issue. L'Angelier might have been attracted to her at the start, but the overriding factor as far as he was concerned was that if he were able to marry her, all that he had ever wished for – money, status and fine living – would be his. He had only to keep Madeleine enamoured and obtain Mr Smith's consent to the marriage, a far more difficult task than he could possibly have imagined.

Madeleine's father was a highly successful architect and an extremely wealthy one, who with his family occupied an elegant house in India Street and a set of offices in Vincent Street. He also owned a country house named Rowaleyn which he had built himself at Row on the Gareloch, some twenty-five miles from Glasgow. With all this came the usual trappings of wealth, such as servants and a carriage and positions on various boards.

Mr Smith had not come by these easily by right of birth and inherited money. The son of a crofter, he had started off by being a builder, and by application to his work he had pulled himself up enough to be considered an eligible young man for the daughter of a famous architect whom he had met in the way of business. The marriage that took place in 1832 had done much to further his career. A somewhat hard-headed businessman, he had no intention of giving his daughter lightly to some opportunist young man with no prospects. When he had learned of L'Angelier's existence and background, he had reacted as one would perhaps expect from someone in his position. Instead of putting an end to the affair, Mr Smith's homily in the drawing room had only made matters worse.

Using Mary Perry as a post lady, and her house as a meeting place, the two lovers conducted their illicit romance with an even greater intensity than before, all the while constantly exchanging love letters. In all, Madeleine wrote 198 love letters that we know of, the constant theme running through all of them being her undying love for L'Angelier.

It has been said that to understand Madeleine Smith you have to read all her letters to L'Angelier. They are the outpourings of a young woman deeply in love, but to anyone reading them, they are merely embarrassing, while giving no deep insight into her character. A letter she wrote as late as the January of 1857 should suffice to give the reader some idea of the tenor of all her letters:

EMILE, MY OWN BELOVED,
You have just left me. Oh, sweet darling, at this moment my heart and soul burns with love for thee; my husband, my own sweet one. Emile, what would I not give at this moment to be your fond wife? We

would be happy. I adore you. I love you with my heart
and soul. I do vex and annoy you, but oh! sweet love,
I do fondly love you with my soul to be your wife,
your own sweet wife . . .

Many of her letters are larded with news of the family
and details of her humdrum existence at home, but all of
them are full of frantic expressions of love, repeated
over and over again until the reading of them soon
begins to pall by the sheer monotony of having to wade
through all the expressions of love in the hope of finding
something of interest about Madeleine herself. What
does come through is her almost slavish submission to
L'Angelier's wishes.

The long delayed moment when the consummation of
their love took place in the May of 1856 in the woods
surrounding their country home seems to have been a
physically painful experience, according to a letter
L'Angelier wrote to Madeleine afterwards, rather than
the moment of sublime ecstasy she had been expecting.
The experience might have been something of a let-
down for her, but her love for L'Angelier remained
undiminished.

L'Angelier, on his part, now felt so sure of her that he
began to show a side of himself that Madeleine had not
seen before. A vain and arrogant man at heart, who
thoroughly subscribed to the Victorian male's tenet that
a woman should be kept in her place, he sent her a list
of resolutions that she should follow. He instructed her
not to go to the Glasgow Ball without his consent, to go
into Sauchiehall Street as little as possible, and in any

case not to go out of the house more than twice a week, to name only a few of the strictures he tried to impose on her.

It was an insensitive letter, written by a shallow and vain man who was now beginning to get above himself, but Madeleine took it like a lamb. Instead of writing a strong letter back, putting him in his place, she wrote back a rather submissive letter, agreeing to most of his terms.

Autumn came and went, and the ominous signs of a bleak Scottish winter were becoming evident when Mr Smith decided he was tired of India Street, and in the November of that year he moved to 5 Blythswood Square, where Mr William Harper Minnoch was one of their neighbours. After he had introduced himself to Mr Smith, and the two men had got talking, Mr Smith was sure that he would make an ideal husband for Madeleine. Minnoch was a man in his early thirties, and was a partner in the firm of Houldsworth and Company. He was well educated, and was always studiously polite to Mr Smith, and much more to the point, he had an income which would allow him to keep his daughter in comfort.

To begin with he made no impression on Madeleine, whose mind was too occupied with thoughts of L'Angelier, whom she still had hopes of marrying. At one period in their relationship, when there had been the possibility of a job for L'Angelier in Lima, she had seriously considered eloping with him, only to abandon the idea after she had given it some thought.

The arrival of William Minnoch was the catalyst that

brought about the end of the affair, a romance which would never have come to anything unless Madeleine had eloped with L'Angelier, when she would have come to rue the day. How could it have been otherwise? She was a well-educated young woman who had recently read Gibbons' *Decline and Fall of the Roman Empire*, and had professed to have actually *enjoyed* reading it. Once the passion that now consumed them both had died, as it inevitably would have done, she would have found herself in the company of an ill-educated womanizer with no money to his name. Something of this may have begun to dawn on her when William Minnoch began to court her.

Gradually, Minnoch's name began to come into her letters to L'Angelier, but not in a way as to give him any suspicions that a rival had appeared on the horizon. He was known to L'Angelier as one of her father's business acquaintances, and from the tone of her letters he would have gathered that she did not greatly care for him.

In a number of ways the move to Blythswood Square was a distinct improvement as far as Madeleine was concerned. L'Angelier's house was only ten minutes' walk away, and in the new house she had chosen for herself a bedroom below ground level which could be reached by a flight of steps. There was no question of L'Angelier sneaking into the bedroom at night as the windows were barred. It did, however, give him easy access to the outside of her window, where he could exchange love letters through the bars, or hold whispered conversations with her while the rest of the house slept.

In the January of the following year, L'Angelier was able to spend a whole hour at the window, whispering his endearments through the bars, while the rest of the house slept. Madeleine seemed equally loving towards him, but there was an odd, almost mechanical note to her responses. If L'Angelier went home that evening feeling that something was wrong, that perhaps their feverish love affair was coming to an end, he would have been right. On 28th January, William Minnoch proposed marriage to Madeleine Smith, as she had been expecting him to do, and she accepted him.

She told L'Angelier nothing of her engagement, but continued to write to him letters that grew increasingly cool and remote, indicating perhaps that their affair would die a natural death. It did not, and at last she wrote the fateful letter that was to set off the train of events which was to lead her to the dock, on trial for her very life.

In her anxiety to get the matter over and done with, she penned a letter and did not mince words. She began:

> You may be astonished at this sudden change – but for some time back you must have noticed a coldness in my notes. My love for you has ceased and that is why I was cool . . .

Towards the end of her letter she brings up the matter of all the love letters she had written him, appealing to him as a man of honour and a gentleman to return them.

L'Angelier was shattered by the news. His beloved 'Mimi' as he was fond of calling her, had suddenly and inexplicably told him that her love for him was over. He wrote back a letter in which grief was compounded by the vindictiveness of a man determined to do as much damage as he could if he was to be denied all his cherished hopes. He not only refused to return the letters, but also threatened to show them to her father.

Madeleine was hysterical with panic, and she promptly wrote back a grovelling letter in which she craved his mercy and humbled herself in a way she should not have done with a man like L'Angelier. She even feigned contrition at her behaviour, asking him to forgive her, and begged him to continue calling at her bedroom window. There was a reconciliation, with L'Angelier playing the role of the magnanimous lover willing to forgive and forget.

It soon became clear to Madeleine that all she had done was to put off the inevitable. L'Angelier was his usual arrogant self again, and was still holding over her head the threat of showing her letters to her father. It was a situation that had to be resolved, and quickly, as she had already agreed to marry Minnoch on 18th June of that year. Madeleine gave the matter some thought and decided there was only one solution to the problem.

On 19th February L'Angelier was taken violently ill with an attack of vomiting and excruciating stomach pains. It is extremely unlikely that this had anything to do with Madeleine, and may well have been the result of stress over their ongoing affair which seemed to be getting nowhere.

In the March, Madeleine made two visits to chemists; one to Murdoch and Son in Sauchiehall Street, where she bought sixpenny-worth of arsenic, for which she signed the poison book, and another at the druggist, Currie, where she bought another ounce of arsenic. This time she was determined to see the last of her lover.

On 21st March, L'Angelier received a letter from her:

Why my beloved did you not come to me Oh beloved are you ill? Come to see me sweet one. I waited and waited for you to come but you did not. I shall wait again tomorrow night same hour and arrangement. Do come my own dear love of a sweetheart. Come beloved and clasp me to your heart. Come and we shall be happy. A kiss fond love. Adieu with tender embraces ever believe me to be your own.

   Ever dear fond
   Mimi

The letter, obviously written at speed, with the writer not even bothering to punctuate, is remarkable for its display of fervent passion by a woman who was about to poison her lover. As such, it needs some beating as an example of how love can be substituted by murderous intent – in this case by a woman who, only a few months before, would have given up everything except her respectability.

The reason that L'Angelier had not come to the basement window for some time was because he had taken a brief holiday at Bridge of Allen, and had arranged for his post to be forwarded to him. When he received Madeleine's letter he was so overjoyed that he returned to Glasgow the same day.

We do not know exactly what transpired when he

arrived at Madeleine's house and went down the basement steps to her window. She had been in the habit of giving him a cup of hot chocolate through the iron bars to keep him warm while he stood forlornly outside. No doubt she did the same this time, plying him with soft words of love while she watched him finish the chocolate, like Lucretia Borgia watching one of her lovers drinking from a poisoned chalice.

One cannot help wondering what her thoughts were after she had sent L'Angelier home that night, knowing he was shortly to die. A feeling of heartfelt relief that she had seen the end of him at last? Or did she perhaps have a sudden attack of remorse as she imagined him being taken violently ill on the walk home, remembering how it had once been between them, as she saw him in her mind's eye staggering down the street with the arsenic gnawing at his innards? From what we know of her, it is more likely that she merely retired to bed and enjoyed a good night's sleep, undisturbed by any bad dreams.

No one came forward at Madeleine Smith's trial to say that they had seen L'Angelier hurrying by the light of the gas lamps to keep his fatal tryst, and no one saw him returning to his lodgings, where his landlady was awakened at 2.30 in the morning by the incessant ringing of the doorbell. She opened it to find L'Angelier writhing in agony in the doorway. Somehow she managed to get him upstairs and into bed, where he complained of feeling cold and asked for an extra blanket and a hot water bottle. These were supplied to him, and from then on he lay quietly in his bed until four o'clock, when his body was racked with another violent spasm.

Now thoroughly alarmed, his landlady went to see Dr James Stevens, who was feeling unwell himself, and merely prescribed laudanum and a mustard poultice, the panacea for most ills in those days it seems. By seven o'clock L'Angelier's condition had worsened and his landlady went to Dr Stevens again, who was by now feeling better. He promised to come shortly but took his time about it, and by the time he arrived he found L'Angelier in a desperate condition.

'It is strange that this is the second time he has gone out well and returned ill,' Dr Stevens murmured, seemingly unperturbed that his patient was obviously dying. 'I must speak and ask him the cause when I visit him again.'

'If I could get some sleep I'm sure I should be better,' L'Angelier said rather pathetically after the doctor had gone. He then asked to see his friend, Miss Perry, giving her address to the landlady.

Miss Perry came almost at once, but by the time she had reached the house, L'Angelier had died. After an emotional scene by the bedside when she kissed L'Angelier on the forehead, Miss Perry dried her tears and hurried round to 5 Blythswood Square, where she saw Mrs Smith. We do not know what transpired between the two women, but whatever was said it was enough to make Mrs Smith retire promptly to her bed after her visitor had gone. Miss Perry had seen Madeleine briefly when she had called at the house, but had said nothing to her of L'Angelier's death. Why not? Was it because she already had her suspicions that L'Angelier had been poisoned?

If she thought of going to the police, the matter was to be taken out of her hands by those more qualified than she to bring the matter before the authorities.

After Miss Perry had left the bedside of the dead man there was a whole flurry of visitors to the house. There was the undertaker come to measure L'Angelier up for his coffin. There was a Dr Thomson, who had been called in by Dr Stevens to see if he could give a reason for the cause of L'Angelier's death. He could supply no answer as to the cause of death, and Stevens therefore declined to issue a death certificate. Of more importance, as events were to turn out, L'Angelier's death had been brought to the attention of his employer, Huggins, who sent Stevenson, the warehouseman, to handle the affairs of the dead man.

Going through his effects, Stevenson found all Madeleine's love letters, and, in his suit pocket, her final note luring him to his death.

'This explains all!' he exclaimed as he read it.

The next day he went to see August De Mean, Chancellor to the French Consul. After he had taken a look at some of the letters and Madeleine's last note, he hurried around to see Mr Smith and showed the letters to him, who was by turns livid with fury that his daughter had been seeing L'Angelier behind his back, and perturbed that she might be involved in something that might need a lot of explaining.

'I know nothing of this man L'Angelier except that at one time she went out with him,' he muttered. 'But I thought I had stopped that relationship months ago.'

'That is hardly my concern,' De Mean murmured.

'But there are certain matters that have to be explained. I would like to ask her a few questions if I may.'

Mr Smith had no option but to agree, and De Mean went on from Smith's offices to Blythswood Square, where he saw Madeleine in the presence of her mother. After informing her that L'Angelier was dead, he wasted no time in coming to the point. He showed her the note. 'Did you see L'Angelier on Sunday night?' he asked.

'I wrote the note last Friday evening,' Madeleine admitted. 'I was hoping that he would come and see me on the Sunday evening. But he did not come.'

She looked at De Mean calmly. 'I swear to you Monsieur De Mean that I have not seen L'Angelier, not on that Sunday, but also not for three weeks – or for six weeks, I am not sure which.'

'The letter you claimed to have written last Friday – why had you arranged a meeting with your former sweetheart when you were engaged to another gentleman?' De Mean asked pointedly.

'I tried to arrange a meeting because I wanted my letters back,' Madeleine told him.

De Mean continued to question her, going over the same questions in an attempt to shake her statement. Each time Madeleine gave him the same answers, and De Mean finally left, convinced she was lying. It would be interesting to know what was said when Mr Smith came home from work that evening. Whatever it was, it was enough to make Madeleine panic and flee from the house the next morning.

In desperation, Mr Smith turned to Minnoch, the one

man he felt he could trust to keep a tactful silence and not attract attention to a situation that seemed to be turning into a major scandal.

'She's probably gone to your country home at Row,' Minnoch said. 'I'll do my best to get her back for you.'

Mr Smith and his wife were still stammering their thanks to Minnoch as he flew out of the house in pursuit of the runaway. No man could have behaved better than he did, given the circumstances. Going by train to Greenock, he was just in time to board the steamer sailing to Helensburgh and Row. Finding Madeleine aboard he gently persuaded her to go back with him to Glasgow, asking nothing in the way of an explanation for her behaviour.

By the time the family went to church on the Sunday, something of what had been happening had already circulated around Glasgow, thanks to L'Angelier's friends, who had been openly speculating on how he had died. When the Smith household walked slowly down the aisle to take their seats in the family pew, their progress was therefore marked with murmuring and whispering which they tried to ignore.

By then Dr Stevens and Dr Thomson had already carried out their postmortem. Their findings were such as to make Thomson feel that it was necessary to hand over to Dr Penny at the Andersonian University a jar containing L'Angelier's stomach. Dr Penny found that the stomach contained eighty-two grains of arsenic, enough to kill several dozen men. Clearly Madeleine had been determined that L'Angelier would not come visiting again.

Minnoch called twice the next week, and on the second occasion Madeleine told him of her relationship with L'Angelier. 'There is talk that he was poisoned, and that I had a hand in his death. I assure you with all my heart this is untrue,' she said. 'It is true that I bought some arsenic for the complexion, but to say that I used it to murder Emile is nonsense.'

'I believe you,' Minnoch said. What else could he say? It was inconceivable anyway that his betrothed was capable of such a crime.

It was the last time he was to speak to her. On the very same day she was arrested by the Procurator Fiscal of Glasgow. As she was not allowed to speak in her defence from the witness box she was allowed to make a declaration before the Sheriff Substitute of Glasgow. In it she freely admitted to her relationship with L'Angelier, but denied any knowledge of his death. As for her purchase of the arsenic, she explained this away as she had done to Minnoch, by saying that she had seen it recommended in an article in a newspaper which had said it was good for the skin, properly diluted in water.

What followed was a form of class warfare in the newspapers, with the *Glasgow Herald* defending its own in an article saying 'that the thought of a highly and virtuously bred young lady could destroy her sweetheart is almost beyond belief', while the gutter press had a field day, adding to the distress of the Smith family by printing the most outrageous lies.

On the morning of 30th June 1857, the trial of Madeleine Smith began at the High Court of Justiciary in Edinburgh. Apart from the general public who sat in the gallery, the case had attracted the attention of some important members of the Scottish clergy and legal profession who sat in the well of the court, trying to ignore the noisy rabble in the gallery who were behaving like a theatre audience waiting for the curtain to go up.

At 10.20 the courtroom was at last silenced by the arrival of the Right Honourable Lord John Hope, the Lord Justice Clark and the Judges Handyside and Ivory. There were a few minutes of expectant silence which rose to a brief buzz of whispered conversations, which were immediately silenced as Madeleine came up from the cells to take her place on the stand. She seemed quite calm as she listened to the charge being read out, and when she replied to it by pleading not guilty, she did so in a quiet, clear voice without a tremor to it.

The prosecution team was headed by the Lord Advocate, James Moncrieff, a man of forty-six who was yet to make his name in his profession, and was therefore intent on making this trial a stepping stone to greater things than he had so far achieved. Against him was ranged John Inglis, who was about the same age as Moncrieff, and who was already Dean of the Faculty of Advocates.

Considering the nature of the case, there were no great clashes between the prosecution and the defence, only the slow marshalling of facts by the prosecution which Inglis tried to rebut. However, the trial did have its dramatic moments when the case against Madeleine Smith seemed to be going against her. One such moment arose from the question of the poison she had purchased. She had told the shop assistant that it was for dealing with rats in the garden, whereas William Campsie, the family gardener, stated quite emphatically, 'I never got any arsenic or poison from Miss Smith to kill rats.'

But the most damning evidence against her came from Mary Perry, who had never really liked Madeleine.

'It's a perfect fascination, my attachment to that girl,' L'Angelier had told her. 'If she were to poison me I would forgive her.'

'Whatever reason would she have to do that?' Miss Perry had asked him.

'I don't know,' L'Angelier had told her. 'Perhaps she might not be sorry to be rid of me.'

This was hardly evidence, but when coupled with another statement from Miss Perry in which she claimed that Madeleine was in the habit of giving cups of chocolate or coffee to L'Angelier, his casual remarks to Miss Perry seemed to be of ominous significance.

The worst moment for Madeleine Smith came when a selection of her love letters were read out in court. But even then the imperturbable calm which she maintained throughout the trial did not desert her. Standing in the dock with an enigmatic Mona Lisa half smile on her lips, she might have been listening to someone reading letters from a stranger for all they seemed to mean to her.

The letters, although branding Madeleine as an adulteress and a liar who had betrayed one of Glasgow's respected citizens, in their way acted in her favour. As Inglis argued in her defence, she must have known that the letters would be discovered and would lead to the very shame and discovery of her affair with L'Angelier, the one thing she dreaded most. No woman would therefore kill her lover in those circumstances, he contended.

Inglis also scored a number of points when he discussed the arsenic that Madeleine was supposed to have administered to her lover. The arsenic that Murdoch's the chemist had sold her was mixed with soot, and the other packet she had obtained from Currie had been mixed with waste indigo. No such colouring matters were found in the body. Moreover, L'Angelier was known to have been an arsenic eater, and he was known to have frequent bouts of stomach trouble – arguments that pointed to L'Angelier having poisoned himself.

Minnoch, who had contributed £500 towards the prisoner's defence, was put into the witness box, where he behaved with his customary decency, in that he never said a single word that might be taken as a criticism of Madeleine. Having appeared at the trial, he then left the court and Madeleine never saw him again. One can hardly blame him.

Throughout the proceedings Madeleine Smith maintained that strange half smile as if the proceedings were such as to be treated with amused contempt. Only during the final speeches for the prosecution and defence did she show any great interest in what was being said.

Moncrieff's address was remarkably restrained, and the main part of it was directed to the arsenic that had been found in the body. 'The fact that no colouring was found in the body,' he said, 'is easily explained. As the deceased had vomited a great deal before his death, no trace of colouring matter would have remained. As for her alleged motive for buying the arsenic, why did she not protest when she found that the powder she had been given was not white?'

Madeleine listened intently to the case for the prosecution leaning against the rail with one hand in which she held a white cambric handkerchief. When she was asked to comment on Moncrieff's address, she said, 'I would like to hear the other side before I comment.' Once again, she seemed to be listening to a case that had nothing to do with her.

When Inglis came to make his speech for the defence, she must have known that he would be fighting for her very life. He did not disappoint her. Unlike Moncrieff, whose address was to the mind, his was to the heart. His speech in her defence lasted for four hours, and remains unsurpassed in the addresses to the courtroom. By the end of it, it became clear to all those present that Madeleine Smith had more than a fair chance of being acquitted.

At twenty-five minutes to two on 9th July 1857, the ninth day of the trial, the jury brought in a verdict of 'Not proven', which allowed her to walk from the court a free woman. The verdict was received with loud cheers and a thunderburst of clapping from the public gallery, where those who had sat through the trial had already decided that she was innocent, thanks to Inglis's masterly speech.

The verdict of 'Not proven', which the jury had given because they thought the evidence was not enough to hang her, inevitably cast a slur on her name, and many newspapers attacked it, saying quite openly that they considered her guilty. *The Scotsman* let it go with the comment that Madeleine was either 'the most fortunate of criminals or the most unfortunate of women'.

As for Madeleine, she rode the storm and married a draughtsman named George Wardle in 1862. When Wardle died in 1910 she went to America where she married a man named Sheehy who died of cancer in 1926. Like Mrs Maybrick, she spent her last years in poverty and died in America in 1928 at the age of ninety-three.

One way and another she had a full life, which is more than can be said for Emile L'Angelier, who had died at the age of thirty-two.

THE ANGEL OF MERCY

Nurse Waddingham (1936)

Poisoners come in many guises. Some, like Dr Crippen, murder for love, others, as in the cases of Adelaide Bartlett and Mrs Maybrick, because they have fallen out of love; they even use poison for the sheer thrill of seeing their victims die, as in the case of Graham Young. The great majority of poisoners, however, have killed for money, and there the list of killers ranges from the mean-spirited, such as Frederick Seddon, to the slightly pathetic and illiterate Charlotte Bryant, and Nurse Dorothea Waddingham, who wasn't a nurse at all, but was in the position to obtain money by killing off two of her patients.

Nurse Waddingham, as she was always called in this case, liked to see herself as an angel of mercy, and if this conjures up a vision of a nurse gliding through the ward and laying a soothing hand on the fevered brow of some of her patients in the manner of Florence Nightingale, it could hardly be applied to Nurse Waddingham.

A slack-jawed and distinctly unprepossessing woman, who was the mother of five children, she had originally come from Hucknall, near Nottingham, where she had been brought up on a small farm owned by her father. After spending some time working in a local factory, she had become a ward maid at the Burton-on-Trent Infirmary. It was while she was working there that she met and married Thomas Leech in 1926. Leech was nearly twice her age and was a sick man when she married him, and it is said that he only worked three months in all the years she was with him. His death from lung cancer, eight years later, harrowing as it was for her, must also have come as a relief, though she was left with four children to bring up alone.

It was during her period with Leech that it became evident that dishonesty came to her easily. She began by walking into a store where she blithely wrote a cheque for £500, which she had no hope of covering. When it bounced she was put on probation for a year. She then took to petty crime as one to the manner born, and was as a result finally sentenced to three years' hard labour.

After her husband's death, her fortunes took an upward swing when she married Ronald Sullivan, who was only three years older than she was, and was something of a war hero as he had been awarded the Military Cross for gallantry on the battlefield.

During the last stages of her first husband's illness, Dorothea Waddingham had decided that she would set up the Waddingham Nursing Home for the elderly and chronically ill. Sullivan's arrival on the scene therefore came at an opportune moment. The two of them moved into 32 Devon Drive, Nottingham, where she assumed the role of Nurse Waddingham, while Sullivan cheerfully undertook all the menial tasks and those of a male nurse.

Unlike Waddingham, Sullivan remains something of a mystery. For that matter, how he ever became involved with her is also somewhat mystifying. An amiable, jug-eared man, one has the feeling that he could have done much better for himself than getting entangled with Waddingham, who was certainly no looker. As it was, she had a child by him within a few months of them going into business, bringing the total to five children they had to bring up. He was probably one of those men who does not ask much from life and is happy to drift along with the tide of events.

Unlike the staff of nursing homes today, who at least have to be approved by the authorities, Nurse Waddingham had no qualifications and employed no one who was a registered nurse. Despite her lack of qualifications, she seems to have been a hard-working woman who made up in part for her lack of nursing skills by looking after her patients to the best of her ability. There was certainly no evidence of her having treated any of her patients badly, as has been brought to light in some instances in recent years. That is if we discount the two patients she killed.

Her problem was one of underfunding. If she had had the capital to create a large and gracious home for the elderly, a tragedy might have been avoided and she would have lived out her life doing a limited amount of good for those who came under her care. As it was, she had no option but to take in whoever came along, however badly she was paid for the services she had to offer.

When Miss Blagg, the Honorary Secretary of the County Nursing Association, came knocking at her door to ask if she was prepared to take in a Mrs Baguley and her daughter, Nurse Waddingham had only one patient staying at the home, and she agreed to take the two women, although they would only be able to pay thirty shillings a week each.

Mrs Baguley turned out to be a small and bent old lady of nearly ninety, while her daughter Ada was a heavily built lady of fifty, who was suffering from progressive disseminated sclerosis which had reached the stage where she was unable to walk or use her arms properly. They were given a ground floor room with two beds in it, so that the mother could get out of bed in the middle of the night in order to adjust her daughter's pillows. It was a tragic situation that had caused a great deal of distress for the father, who had tried to cope with his daughter's terrifying illness until his death in 1925, when Mrs Baguley had continued to look after her daughter, despite her great age. At last, however, they had reached a haven where they could end their days in a peace of sorts, given the circumstances.

As may be imagined, Ada was a difficult person to nurse, and had already knocked over a light in the bedroom and set light to the furnishings. Trying to cope with this difficult couple without staff, save herself and Sullivan, to say nothing of having to bring up her children, began to get Nurse Waddingham down, and she began to complain bitterly about the money she was paid by the Baguleys, who, needless to say, were well satisfied with the arrangement, as well they might be. Mrs Baguley, who seems to have been an indomitable old lady, was particularly happy there, and quite content to see the remaining years of her life slip by pottering around the garden or watching the traffic go by the front gate.

Towards the end of February 1935, Waddingham was unfortunate enough to lose her other patient, Miss Kemp, who had been under treatment by Dr Manfield, who had been prescribing morphine tablets for her. This

left Waddingham with an income of three pounds a
week from the Baguleys, who were living there for
practically nothing after she had fed them and kept them
warm through the winter months. She said nothing, but
grimly soldiered on, looking after her two remaining
patients, one of whom was now so ill that she had to be
dressed and undressed.

The one worry the Baguleys had was the fear that
Nurse Waddingham would refuse to keep them, at which
point they would have to go into the County Hospital,
which would immediately create financial difficulties. In
her will, Ada had left most of her money to her faithful
fiancé, Frederick Gilbert, who had remained deeply
attached to her through the years, though her lingering
illness had put an end to the possibility of them ever
marrying.

Nurse Waddingham was now getting desperate for
money, and she put to Ada the suggestion that in
exchange for making over all her property to her, she in
turn would undertake to look after Ada and her mother
for the rest of their lives.

It was a poor deal to begin with as neither woman had
all that long to live, but Ada was anxious to see that they
were not thrown out, and she agreed to Nurse Waddingham's suggestion. Her solicitor was appalled at the idea
and tried to persuade her against such a foolish action,
pointing out that once she was no longer in control of
her money, she could still land up in the workhouse
infirmary. A compromise was finally worked out
between them, in which Ada was to make out a new will
in Waddingham's favour, rather than handing over

everything to her right away, and on 4th May the new will was drawn up, when Sullivan was brought into it by being named as an equal beneficiary.

Everything then proceeded normally at the Waddingham Home until 12th May, when Mrs Baguley suddenly died. Ada attended the funeral in a wheelchair pushed by Sullivan. There she briefly met Frederick Gilbert, her former fiancé, who had visited her occasionally at the home. It was a poignant moment, meeting again the man she had once been engaged to more than twenty years ago. Perhaps even worse for her was having to go back alone to the room she had once shared with her mother. Now, for the first time in her life she was really alone, and had she but known it, completely at the mercy of Nurse Waddingham, who had no intention of allowing Ada to remain alive longer than was necessary.

On 10th September, Ada had a visit from a Mrs Briggs, who had been a friend of the family for more than thirty years. She found Ada as well as could be expected in the circumstances, and when she left she promised to come back the following Thursday and take her home with her for tea. It had been a beautiful September day, and Ada went to bed that night in a happier frame of mind than usual. By one o'clock in the moming she was dead, after having suddenly gone into a coma late at night.

For someone who had just lost one of her patients, Nurse Waddingham did not seem unduly upset. This was really hardly surprising, as she was now about to inherit the best part of £2,000, plus the proceeds of the sale of Ada's house, more than enough to keep her afloat until better days came along for the nursing home.

If Nurse Waddingham had left it at that, and had allowed Ada to be buried in the normal way, she might well have got off scot free. Instead, she forged a letter purporting to be from Ada requesting that she should be cremated after her death. The second piece of sheer stupidity that would inevitably draw suspicion to her was when she went on to state in the letter, 'It is my last wish that my relatives shall not know of my death.'

For someone to leave instructions for their body to be' cremated was very unusual at a time when cremations were a rare occurrence, and she had been a conventional-minded person anyway, so that such a request was enough in itself to cause suspicion. Coupled with her request that relatives should not be informed, suspicion must have amounted to near certainty, as it did in the mind of Dr Cyril Banks, Medical Officer for Health for Nottingham, and the crematorium referee. As soon as he received the letter he ordered a postmortem. This was carried out by Dr Taylor, senior assistant to the Nottingham City Analyst, who found that the body contained more than three grains of morphine.

The discovery that the cause of death was due to Ada being administered an overdose of morphine, and not from a cerebral haemorrhage, inevitably led to the suspicion that her mother might also have died from the same cause.

This discovery led to the exhumation of Mrs Baguley's remains, and an autopsy was carried out by Dr Roche Lynch, who was to play an important part in the murder trial of Charlotte Bryant only three months later.

His findings were equally as damning in this case as they were to be for Bryant. Mrs Baguley had also died of morphine poisoning. The day after the body had been exhumed, Frederick Gilbert committed suicide, adding a sad footnote to Ada Baguley's tragic life.

In the January of 1936, Detective Inspector Pentland arrived at the home with a warrant for the arrest of Nurse Waddingham and Sullivan. Because the evidence against them for the murder of Mrs Baguley was tenuous, they were arrested only on the charge of poisoning Ada Baguley.

All murder cases in those days, when persons found guilty of murder were mostly hanged, attracted far more attention than they do today. The abolition of the death penalty has taken much of the drama out of a murder case for a public who once treated a murder trial as a form of entertainment – better even than going to the pictures. Those who were unable to attend read all about it in the newspapers. The trial of Nurse Waddingham and Sullivan was no exception. Banner headlines, and opinions as to their guilt or otherwise, were freely aired in the columns of the more popular press before Waddingham and Sullivan had even come to trial, in the February of 1936 at the Nottingham Assizes, where they were charged jointly with the murder of Ada Baguley.

When the trial began the press had already tied the noose around their necks. Now all that was left was for the judge and jury to see that the due process of law, as the press happened to see it, was carried out.

The public prosecutor in this case was the famous Norman Birkett, while the defence was to be conducted by J. F. Eales, MP and Recorder of Nottingham. Considering that he was up against one of the greatest lawyers the English bar has ever known, he was to do better than expected in what was basically a hopeless case. Justice Goddard was the judge in this trial.

In past murder cases it was often fairly obvious from the start that the accused was guilty as charged. Brilliant defence lawyers such as Marshall Hall sometimes managed to persuade the jury otherwise in the face of all the evidence, and their guilt or innocence still remained a matter of private speculation. In this case, Nurse Waddingham's guilt was never really in doubt from the beginning, and to make her fate a certainty, she had no brilliant defence lawyer to save her, even though Eales did his best. Ronald Sullivan was another matter again. Early in the trial Birkett tried to establish that Sullivan was a party to the murder, only to be informed by the judge that in his opinion there was no case for Sullivan to answer. He leaned forward in his chair as if to emphasize the point he was about to make. 'The only evidence that has come out against Sullivan is that he may have been a participant, not that he must have been.'

Birkett tried to disagree, but Justice Goddard brushed his protests aside. 'In my judgement,' he told both counsels, 'there is not sufficient evidence in this case to justify me leaving the case against Sullivan to the jury.' After a formal verdict of 'Not guilty' had been recorded, Sullivan was allowed to leave the court a free man, leaving Nurse Waddingham to face alone the awful majesty of the court which would send her to the gallows if she were found guilty.

If Justice Goddard had not intervened at that point, Sullivan would have remained on trial for his life, and there is no telling what the outcome would have been, a jury's reaction to a prisoner being one of the unreliable factors in a murder case, as the prejudices of a judge can also be. Nor does the prosecutor always play fair. Sometimes a court of law becomes little more than an arena for a deadly game played out between the prosecutor and the counsel for the defence, with the judge having the final word. In this case, Sullivan was lucky to have a judge who was anxious to see that justice was done.

To be fair to Birkett, he had already said that there was no direct evidence against Sullivan for either possession or administration of morphine. Having said that, it is surprising he bothered to argue with the judge's decision to free Sullivan.

Even after Sullivan had left the courtroom, the judge saw to it that Birkett did not have it all his own way, carefully pointing out from time to time anything that might stand in Nurse Waddingham's favour. But the evidence as to her guilt was still undeniable. The most damning evidence came during Birkett's examination of Dr Manfield.

'Did you at any time prescribe medicine with morphine in it?' he asked the doctor.

'I did not,' Dr Manfield said emphatically.

'Did you leave with anybody at Devon Drive any morphine other than that you left for Miss Kemp (Waddingham's only other patient)?'

'No.'

Nurse Waddingham's only defence was that Dr Manfield *had* left morphine tablets with her for Ada. 'I administered morphine to Ada Baguley in accordance with the doctor's instructions, who left the tablets for that purpose,' she said.

'There was never occasion for the use of morphine tablets in the case of Ada Baguley,' Dr Manfield snapped. 'I never gave them. I never prescribed them.'

In all the questions that were put to Waddingham relating to the administration of morphine to Ada, it came down in the end to whose words the jury would accept, and it was obvious by their expressions who they believed.

Waddingham's case was not helped when Miss Blagg from the County Nursing Association took the stand and told the court of a conversation that had occurred between the two women on one of her frequent visits to the home. Nurse Waddingham had told Miss Blagg that Ada was going to hand over her money to her.

'Hand over her money to you!' Miss Blagg had exclaimed. 'Her body is in a bad state, but her mind is all right.'

'It won't be for long,' Nurse Waddingham had replied with a sour smile.

'She was distinctly abusive to me,' Miss Blagg said indignantly. She glared at Waddingham as she told the court how the nurse had threatened to send Mrs Baguley and her daughter to Basford, the local Poor Law Institution. 'I shall write to Basford tonight and they shall go tomorrow,' she had said menacingly.

No one who was put on the witness stand had a good word to say for Nurse Waddingham. Mrs Wood, an old friend of the Baguleys, told how she had visited them at least a dozen times and had only been able to see them once alone. A cousin named Louisa Taylor repeated a statement she had made at the magistrates' hearing, when she had told the chairman that the nurse had told her that Ada had made over her money to them, a remark that provoked a violent outburst from Nurse Waddingham who had cried out, 'Don't be such a liar.' This time she said nothing.

Mrs Briggs' evidence was even more damaging. According to her, Nurse Waddingham had informed her that she had already given Ada four morphine tablets to deaden her pain. Apart from anything else, this would have made her drowsy and not inclined to talk, whereas she had been bright and cheerful, Mrs Briggs maintained. Nurse Waddingham denied this. 'Ada was poorly all that day,' she said. 'She had pains after dinner and I gave her two more tablets. When Mrs Briggs left she told me that Ada was in great pain and I had better go to her.'

It was pointed out by the judge in his summing up that if Ada had been in great pain that day, how was it that she had been given a heavy meal only the day before? He referred to a list of the meals that Nurse Waddingham had given the judge, and then looked up. 'Can you, as men of common sense, think that anybody in their senses would give a woman suffering from such sharp abdominal pains that morphia had to be given for three nights, two helpings of pork, roast potatoes and fruit pie?'

In the face of this, Eales had an almost non-existent hand to play, but there were a few points in Nurse Waddingham's favour, and he made the most of them. 'There was no secrecy about the will,' he told the court. At one point in the trial Nurse Waddingham had elected to go into the witness box and Eales was quick to point out how co-operative she had been in this case. 'When Detective Inspector Pentland called at Devon Drive she said, "I will tell you anything I know and assist you in every way." Even after listening to all the evidence she did not shrink from entering the witness box,' he said, pointing a finger at Nurse Waddingham, who was doing her best to look an innocent woman and not making a very good job of it.

When it came to the summing up, the judge also made a few points in her favour, pointing out that the Baguleys had not been lured into coming to the home, but had come of their own free will. 'There is also ample evidence that the Baguleys were comfortable and well cared for,' he said.

However, an acknowledgement that Nurse Waddingham had not sought out the Baguleys and had run the home efficiently was hardly relevant when it came to making a decision as to whether or not she was guilty. After being out for more than two hours the jury returned with a verdict of 'Guilty' with a strong recommendation for mercy.

'I am innocent,' Nurse Waddingham said, staring wildly around the court as she tried to face the dreadful implications of the verdict. Unlike some murderers who had marked their last appearance before the public with a display of histrionics, Nurse Waddingham left, still looking dazed, as if she had not fully realized that she was soon to die on the gallows.

Despite the jury's appeal for mercy, Nurse Waddingham was hanged at Winson Green Prison, Birmingham, on 16th April 1936, after appointing Sullivan to act as guardian to her children.

By a strange irony of fate, her solicitor had approached Norman Birkett to defend her, but as it happened, the Crown had already appointed him. If he had appeared for her, the outcome of the trial may well have been vastly different.